CURIOUS WALKS
AROUND
LONDON

CURIOUS WALKS
AROUND
LONDON

DAVID BRANDON & ALAN BROOKE

AMBERLEY

First published 2011

Amberley Publishing Plc
Cirencester Road, Chalford,
Stroud, Gloucestershire, GL6 8PE

www.amberley-books.com

British Library Cataloguing in Publication Data.
A catalogue record for this book is available from the British Library.

ISBN 978 1 4456 0294 3

Typeset in 10 point on 12 point Celeste Pro.
Typesetting and Origination by Amberley Publishing.
Printed in the UK.

Contents

Introduction

The purpose of this book is to provide what is hopefully an informative and entertaining selection of walks around well-known and some less-visited parts of London. We make no attempt to replicate the many excellent earlier or existing publications which guide people round the streets of the metropolis in search of ghostly or criminal associations, for example, or architectural features. Rather, while there may indeed be passing allusions to supernatural or illegal activities and to interesting buildings, we intend to concentrate on oddities, curiosities, strange stories, bizarre connections or those things to be seen in the streets which are so familiar that they are frequently simply overlooked. The seemingly mundane or the understated can often on investigation turn out to be as fascinating as the best-known of London's historic monuments.

The authors make no apology for their love of and perennial enthusiasm for London and its history. As callow youths they wandered the streets, keen to find out what was round the corner and rarely disappointed, revelling in the sheer complexity and diversity which are such features of the capital. Remaining callow but sadly no longer so youthful, they are still on the streets and never happier than when grubbing around obscure alleys or coming across some serendipitous curiosity of the sort largely unseen by those with more urgent and important demands on their time.

The walks suggested here are the personal and entirely subjective choices of the authors and we hope that our readers will find them rewarding. These walks have in common an attempt to highlight the curiosity and diversity that have been mentioned but we also know that for each of the walks that are included, dozens of others that would offer up an alternative harvest of eclectic delights could also be included. We do not stray far out of what can loosely be described as 'central London'.

Any opinions expressed are the authors' own highly subjective judgements. On the other hand, where we provide information we hope we have the facts right or at least provide some acknowledgement where there is any doubt. Parts of London are changing extremely rapidly and when the authors revisited these walks in April and May 2010, they found some familiar sights had changed or gone for good. Time and tide and all that ... so by the time this book appears in print, doubtless there will have been more changes.

1

Borough and
a Bit of Bermondsey

The authors felt that this shortish walk was particularly relevant given the extraordinary transformation that is currently taking place between Borough High Street and Tower Bridge Road.

Historically, the Borough has been part of Southwark, transpontine London, for as long as London itself and the bridge over the Thames have existed. Roads to London from the Channel ports and the towns along the south coast converged on what is now Borough High Street. This then channelled the traffic through to London Bridge and across to the City. It was always a cosmopolitan, unsettled quarter, many of the people lodging or living in the district essentially being on their way, sooner or later, to somewhere else. This transient activity was characterised by a large number of inns, traces of which can still be seen. London Bridge was closed at night and so travellers who arrived in the late evening often had little choice but to find accommodation. Many of the coaches were too wide for the congested London Bridge and so the practice of terminating coaches at these inns was encouraged.

The Borough came to house a sizeable immigrant community and successive generations of immigrants established industries in the locality. A very wide and eclectic range of industries developed before the nineteenth century. Prominent among these was brewing. Settlers from the Low Countries introduced beer to England. Beer contained hops and gradually replaced the un-hopped traditional English ales. Large quantities of hops were cultivated in Kent, not far away. Most businesses were small in scale and clothing. The making of hats and the leather trade were particularly prominent but metal-working and victualling also provided much employment. Glass-making was also an industry associated with the district.

In the Victorian period the Borough and the part of Bermondsey that we are visiting became a noxious, polluted and overcrowded mix of dire working-class housing and industry, much of which involved food-processing. It became known as 'London's Larder', the raw materials for which mostly arrived at the riverside wharves and were distributed from the warehouses which were such a feature of the district. As organic changes took place in the nature of the British economy and also in the size of ships and the way in which the shipping industry operated, the wharves and warehouses became obsolete and the associated industries declined. By the 1980s the northern parts of Southwark had become a kind of underbelly to London with dereliction and inner-city decline and decay – all just a stone's throw from the gilded temples of mammon in the City.

Within the last decade or so the district has been undergoing a transformation. It began in 2000 with the opening of Tate Modern in nearby Bankside since when developments such as the reconstruction of Shakespeare's Globe Theatre and the opening of the Millennium Bridge have assisted the reinvention of the district as a prime site for offices, expensive apartments, chic eating places and tourist attractions. This inevitably means that the character of Borough and Bankside is changing very rapidly and further development plans will only accelerate that process. It is as if multinational Big Business has suddenly discovered a previously ignored prime location ripe for exploitation right on the doorstep of the City of London and is now homing in gleefully and greedily to make the most of it. Social polarization is an inevitable outcome.

The Walk

From London Bridge main line or tube station via Railway Approach, turn left into Borough High Street. Walk down the east side of the street. Immediately on the left is a grey stone-like building seemingly out of place in these surroundings. This was part of St Thomas' Hospital and is now a post office. It bears a Borough of Southwark plaque indicating that the first Bible printed in English was produced on this site. The year was 1537. It should be remembered that it took great courage to print and publish such a work at that time in the face of the terror imposed by the Catholic Church, which did not want the word of God made more accessible by being printed in a language other than Latin.

Another Borough of Southwark plaque explains that St Thomas' Hospital was founded on this site in 1225, rebuilt in 1552 and relocated in 1865. Caution is sometimes needed with the 'facts' displayed on London's plaques. Early in the fifteenth century, Richard Whittington, the eminent Lord Mayor of London, established a small hostel on this site for those who later came to be known as 'fallen women'. This gained the reputation of being a bawdy house whose master enjoyed the services of concubines. Hospitals were rough-and-ready establishments before the reforms of the nineteenth century. Drunkenness was rife among patients and carers and the authorities at St Thomas' had to draw up rules to ensure that there was only one patient per bed and that patients did not enter wards allocated to the opposite sex. They went to considerable lengths to exclude patients with infectious diseases or those who seemed to be incurable. Much of the site of St Thomas' disappeared under the huge London Bridge Station and the hospital moved to magnificent new premises close to Westminster Bridge.

Pass St Thomas Street on the left (we will return soon) and the short stretch to Newcomen Street is punctuated by small entries. These bear such names as: King's Head Yard, White Hart Yard, George Inn Yard, Talbot Yard and Queen's Head Yard. These names are evidence of the Borough's role in providing hospitality and accommodation for those travelling to and from London. Some of these establishments dated back to medieval times and most were still trading in the mid-nineteenth century after which they succumbed to the competition of the railways.

Only one of these yards shows much sign of its past and it is of course that which contains the illustrious George Inn. It is likely that an inn was established on this site in the Middle Ages. A sixteenth-century replacement was burned down in the Great Fire of Southwark in 1676 and what can be seen today is one surviving wing of that seventeenth-century building. It is remarkable for being the only survivor of the galleried inns, of which London once had dozens, although sadly its other two wings were demolished in the nineteenth century. The George which, like the whole district, has Dickensian connections, belongs to the National Trust. Talbot Yard was the location

The George Inn, Borough High Street.

of the most famous of Southwark's ancient inns. This was the Tabard, immortalised as the inn which Chaucer makes the starting point for his pilgrims in the *Canterbury Tales.* On the gable end of No. 161 a ghost advertisement promotes the services of 'The Monster Ready Made & Bespoke Clothing Establishment'.

Newcomen Street contains the King's Arms pub. Its façade displays a fine sign which was removed from the southern gateway of Old London Bridge in 1760. Newcomen Street takes its name from Mrs Jonathon Newcomen, who in 1675 left money for charitable work in the neighbourhood. The street is actually the opening up and widening of yet another inn yard, this having once been the Axe & Bottle. At No. 9 a privately erected plaque commemorates John Marshall, who died in 1637 and left money for the care of old churches.

Chapel Court is an easy-to-miss entry which on its north side shows evidence of the antiquity of some of the buildings in the High Street. This building has a brick façade to the High Street but its back reaches show timber framing and plasterwork covering the infill, possibly dating to the sixteenth century.

Turn left into Angel Place and you will see what is still a forbidding portion of the wall of the former Marshalsea Prison. This dated back to the fourteenth century and tended to house debtors and those who had held people in authority up to ridicule. The Marshalsea closed in 1842. At the junction of the High Street with Long Lane and Marshalsea Road stands the church of St George the Martyr. There was certainly a church on this site in the twelfth century but what can be seen now is mostly from a second rebuilding in the 1730s. The tower makes its contribution to the list of London's oddities because the clock in the tower has a dial showing on each side but only three of them are illuminated in the hours of darkness. The lighted ones face the Borough; the unlit one faces towards Bermondsey because, if the story is to be believed, those who lived in that district refused to contribute towards the cost of rebuilding the church in the eighteenth century. There are close associations between this church and Charles Dickens's novel *Little Dorrit.*

We retrace our steps up the High Street and turn right into St Thomas Street. On the north side is the Old Operating Theatre and Herb Garrett. This is a museum recalling those fearsome days when surgery was carried out on the traumatized patient without anaesthetics and without antiseptics. Paying for the vicarious enjoyment of gory terrors was a feature of this part of Southwark with the London Dungeon close by in Tooley Street. The Old Operating Theatre is the only surviving example in the UK of a nineteenth-century location where operations were carried out before science started to come to the assistance of the surgeon and, of course, the patient. Adjacent to the Old Operating Theatre is the former church of St Thomas' and it was in the loft of the church that the herbs used to make medicines were stored and dried.

In April 2010, looming above and grossly out of scale with poor old St Thomas Street, a concrete stump was under construction which will form the lower core of the 'Shard of Glass' or Shard London Bridge as it will be officially known. When it is completed in 2012, this will be the tallest building in Europe at 310 metres. Described in the planners' blurb as 'an inspirational mixed use urban village concept', this will be without doubt a building of stunning visual impact, even a kind of beauty. Whether it

Marshalsea Prison

Beyond this old wall is the site of the old Marshalsea Prison, closed in 1842. This sign is attached to a remnant of the prison wall. Charles Dickens, whose father had been imprisoned here for debt in 1824, used that experience as the Marshalsea setting for his novel Little Dorrit.

HISTORIC SOUTHWARK

Plaque marking the site of Marshalsea Prison.

will serve any really useful purpose other than to make some exceedingly rich people even richer is doubtful. However, it cannot be all bad because one requirement of its erection is the demolition of Southwark Towers next door. This is, or was, a gross excrescence comprising twenty-four storeys of office space which in 2010 was coming down just as rapidly as 'The Shard' was going up. This book attempts to consider what may loosely be described as 'curiosities' and 'oddities' of London. It is perhaps fair to say that when complete, 'The Shard' with its extraordinary height and appearance will constitute a visual curiosity much in the way that the 'Gherkin' in the City already does. This has certainly inspired affection in the relatively few years that it has been a feature of the skyline. The authors, however, feel that it is the serendipitous discoveries to be made while walking London's streets that are generally more rewarding.

To recover some sense of sanity, we cross to the south side of St Thomas Street and enter an arcade and courtyards which compose most of the original buildings of Guy's Hospital. This was founded in 1722 by Thomas Guy (1645–1724). Guy was the son of a coal merchant and he ostensibly became rich through developing a very successful bookselling business. The story is told that he was a natural miser. He was engaged to

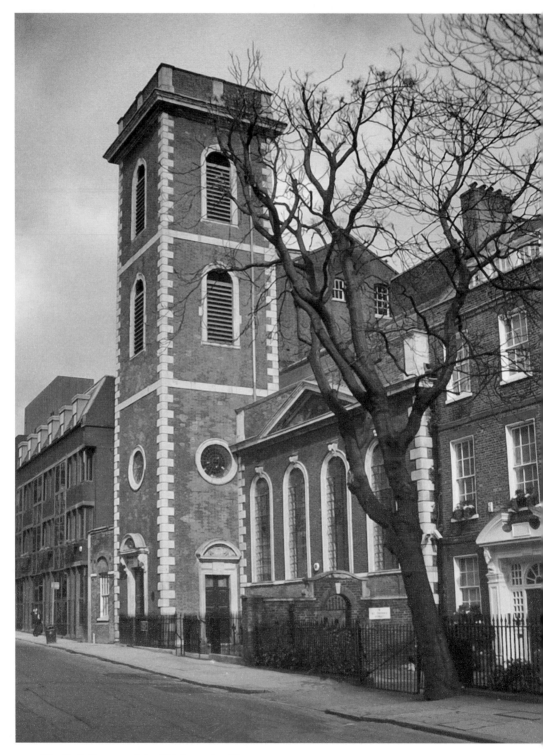

The Herb Garret and the Old Operating Theatre.

Shard London Bridge under construction in April 2010.

marry a woman much younger than himself. His house needed various repairs before the nuptials took place. These were badly bodged and his wife-to-be, Sally, without his authority, drew on his account to pay for expensive rectification. Guy was so horrified by what he regarded as her profligate spending that he broke off the engagement and resolved to remain a bachelor till his dying day. He kept his resolve, making sure that he kept his hands on the purse-strings. Guy did not really make his millions very ethically. In the eighteenth century, merchant seamen were often paid in promissory notes redeemable at a later date. He bought these at a considerable discount from sailors who needed ready money and he cashed them later at their full value. The only generosity he ever showed was endowing the founding of the hospital to the tune of £238,292. The hospital when it opened was state-of-the-art but it teaches us

Plaque to Thomas Guy, founder of Guy's Hospital.

Shelter from Old London Bridge at Guy's Hospital.

something of the state of patient care at that time to learn that in 1735 a man was employed full-time to destroy the bed bugs that plagued the place. The old buildings are delightful and include a statue of Thomas Guy himself. An oddity close by is one of the alcoves from Old London Bridge which had been demolished in 1830. These allowed pedestrians some relief from the danger of injury or worse resulting from the permanent pandemonium that was the traffic on that heavily congested bridge.

Return to St Thomas Street and continue until turning right into Weston Street and then left into Snowsfields. Here can be seen model workers' dwellings erected by the Guinness Trust, which was set up by Sir Edward Guinness in 1890. From Snowsfields turn right into Bermondsey Street. This is now a conservation area and retains vestiges of a village feel. The street led to the major Cluniac monastery of Bermondsey Abbey, of which very little trace can be seen above ground. Abbey Street stands on the site of the nave and the crossing was at the present junction of Abbey Street and Tower Bridge Road. In Grange Walk off Grange Road, which is just outside the designated area for this stroll, can be seen a small group of gabled buildings recognisable as part of a late medieval gatehouse.

There is a ghost advertisement on the side of 57 Bermondsey Street and some old bowed shop fronts from Nos 68 to 72. No. 78 has a bow window at first-floor level and weatherboarding in a vernacular style. The Garrison pub has an old etched glass window. No. 189 has a curious carved lintel inscribed 'Time & Talents Settlement 1907'. This organisation was an early example of community self-help and initiated many projects over the years which benefited what was for long a deprived neighbourhood. At the south end of the street, the church of St Mary Magdalen is a visual curiosity. This church, which was founded in 1290, served the settlement that had developed around the Abbey. Most of the fabric that can be seen dates from the rebuilding of the late seventeenth century but what is striking is the quaint west front in what can best be described as a freelance but lovable Gothic Revival style. It was erected by a local architect in 1830. An odd little watch-house stands at the corner of Abbey Street.

Return along Bermondsey Street, turn left and proceed straight ahead into Leathermarket Street. The name of this street and of Tanner Street and Morocco Street nearby are reminders that this was the centre of London's leather-processing industry, dating back to the thirteenth or fourteenth centuries. Typically this was the kind of noxious industry that the City of London authorities did not want on their doorstep. So, along with many other polluting industries, it was consigned to across the river, but not too far away, in this case Bermondsey. But the adjacent Borough and Bankside districts also became a major industrial enclave from the Middle Ages right through

Insignia of the Guinness Trust.

until the 1970s and 1980s. The presence of hoists at roof level in the trendy apartments that are such a feature of this quarter is evidence that so many of these buildings were formerly used as warehouses and other types of industrial premises.

Turn left into Weston Street. On the left will be seen the Bermondsey Leather Market. This was built in 1879. It and the adjacent Leather Exchange were saved from demolition in 1993 and turned into modern workspaces. Return along Weston Street and turn right into Snowsfields. Cross the junction of Tooley Street and Bermondsey Street and go ahead along Crucifix Lane. The Rood or Cross of Bermondsey Abbey was a lucrative asset for that monastery because it was venerated by large numbers of pilgrims. Shortly after its dissolution in 1539, the Abbey was bought by Sir Thomas Pope who erected the Rood at the east end of this street, which was later renamed Crucifix Lane. The Crucifix itself was soon removed in these vehemently anti-Catholic times and was destroyed a few years later.

Crucifix Lane joins Druid Street which then makes a junction with Tooley Street. On the north side of Tooley Street two statues may be seen, close to each other. Although unexceptional in themselves, they constitute something of a curiosity because of the consonance of the names of the two men being commemorated. One is Colonel Samuel Bourne Bevington (1832–1907) and the other, depicted more in a bust than a statue, is Ernest Bevin (1881–1951). Bevington's wealth came from the local leather industry and he was the first mayor of Bermondsey. Bevin was a tough East Ender who made a name for himself as a trade union organiser and went on to became a leading Labour politician.

There are views of Tower Bridge to die for at this point. This iconic bridge qualifies as a curiosity because it employed the very latest technology but disguised its mechanical hardware in two mock-Gothic towers. Close by is one of London's very oddest-looking buildings and one which makes a piquant contrast to the bridge. This is City Hall. It may look like a slightly tipsy curled up woodlouse but we are assured that it leans the way it does in order to maximise its energy efficiency. This is easier to believe than the claim that its extensive use of glass symbolises the transparency of the political decisions and processes that take place within. It comes from the Foster & Partners stable that has given us a number of other eye-catching and innovative buildings of late. Irreverent people have been heard to call this building 'The Mayor's Testicle'.

Going back towards London Bridge along Tooley Street, on the north side at No. 33, one of the oldest commemorative plaques in London can be seen. This remembers James Braidwood, who was the highly regarded Superintendent of the London Fire Brigade. He died supervising operations to contain the great fire that devastated the Tooley Street warehouses in 1861. On this occasion the Thames became a river of fire as containers of such highly flammable items as molasses, sugar, and various kinds of oil, exploded in the heat and their burning contents oozed into the water. St Olaf House shows some fine art deco features. London Bridge tube and main line stations are just across the road to complete the walk.

Tower Bridge.

City Hall.

Plaque to James Braidwood, Cottons Lane at the corner of Tooley Street.

2

Whitechapel and Stepney

This walk takes us through parts of the borough of Tower Hamlets. We are bounded by Aldgate and Leman Street on the west, Cable Street on the south, Stepney Green on the east and Whitechapel High Street, Whitechapel Road and Mile End Road on the north.

This is very much London's East End. It is a pulsating, culturally diverse and cosmopolitan district of immense historical interest and great character, if sometimes slightly intimidating, rundown and weary. It is hard and uncompromising and it has managed to retain a distinct identity, despite experiencing so much destruction in the Second World War and developing pockets of gentrification since then. By today's standards it exhibits much deprivation and social exclusion. The contrast with the untold billions of pounds wrapped up in the glitzy offices of the City so close by simply could not be greater. Much of what we will see is well off the usual tourist radar. We don't believe that it is any the less interesting for that.

This area, being close to the Thames and the Pool of London – in the nineteenth century the greatest port in the world – has traditionally catered for the needs of mariners. It contained brothels, eating places, louche drinking dens and other dives aimed at enticing the money out of the pockets of newly paid sailors. Huge numbers of jobs were to be had in the docks but many of them were casual and so the dockworkers and their families needed to live close to the dock gates. Again, this part of the inner East End, being near the river, was a natural first settling place for successive waves of immigrants. Many arrived with little more than the clothes they were wearing and took the cheapest and worst accommodation nearby. They frequently brought their skills with them, and the East End developed an extraordinarily wide range of trades, often on a very small scale and with appalling working conditions – truly the 'sweated industries'. Other industries that developed often depended on the presence of the docks for their imported raw materials and the export of their finished products. These were often industries that produced noxious effluents and polluted the atmosphere so the City of London's powerful élite did not want them too near the 'Square Mile'.

In the nineteenth century, Britain had a fairly liberal and tolerant political system compared to many tyrannical regimes elsewhere in Europe. Britain was for fifty years or so the leading industrial and manufacturing nation in the world. She was extremely rich, even though the wealth was shared out very unequally. For these reasons, London attracted large numbers of immigrants who came as refugees to escape political and religious persecution or as economic migrants looking to better their prospects. It frequently took them a generation or two to do so.

Successive waves of immigrants arrived in the London docks and naturally tended to settle close by. Among the immigrants were Ashkenazi Jews from Russia and Eastern Europe and Sephardic Jews mainly from Spain and Portugal. They brought with them their own languages, food, religions and culture and, united in poverty, they tended to huddle closely together in their own communities for mutual support and defence. Large numbers of Irish people settled, many of them escaping the crushing despair associated with the so-called Potato Famine of the 1840s. Their presence was resented because it was believed that they formed a pool of cheap labour, forcing wages down. Around what is now Royal Mint Street (it used to be called Rosemary Lane), a sizeable German community developed, many of the men working in local sugar refineries.

We could go on. The indigenous population and the new arrivals lived in close proximity. Occasionally, tensions rose to the surface with fights and riots occurring, but generally the experience of shared deprivation led to a rough-and-ready toleration. The East End gained a reputation for bad housing, a blighted environment, for poverty and criminality. It was described by one social investigator in the 1890s in the following terms:

> The East End is a city without a centre – an area where every service and commodity essential to civilised life is lacking: sewerage and drainage were so inadequate that the smell of decay and disease constantly pervaded the streets; streets and alleys were so badly lit that the pickpockets, thugs and murderers could lurk undetected in the dim courtyards...

Another writer noted that 'the lodgings here are occupied by dredgers, ballast heavers, coal whippers, watermen, lumpers and others whose trade is connected with the river ... The poverty of these workers compels them to lodge wherever the rent is lowest.'

The Walk

Leave Aldgate or Aldgate East tube stations and turn east along the north side of Whitechapel High Street and continue into Whitechapel Road. Whitechapel was an early suburb of the City and the road was the main route out towards Essex and East Anglia. The eponymous 'White Chapel' became a parish church in the fourteenth century, was rebuilt many times, and then largely destroyed in the Blitz. On the north side off the High Street, down Angel Alley, is a left-wing bookshop outside which there is a mural bearing images of heroes of the movement. Close by at Gunthorpe Street, above a shop, is a coat of arms with the Star of David, evidence of the former large-scale Jewish presence in the district. The offices of the now defunct *Jewish Daily News* were located here. At No. 80 is the Whitechapel Art Gallery, opened in 1901. This has a striking Art Nouveau frontage. Close to the library is a blue plaque to Isaac Rosenberg (1890–1918). The son of Russian Jews who emigrated to Britain, he became a painter and poet who was killed serving on the Somme. Recognition that his work was on a par with better-known war poets, such as Wilfred Owen and Siegfried Sassoon, seems to have come largely posthumously.

No. 259 Whitechapel Road is a shop in which John Merrick, nicknamed 'The Elephant Man', was exhibited in the 1880s among a group of human freaks. The woebegone man suffered from a condition which meant that he looked like a pachyderm. Merrick was a gentle and sensitive man who only wanted to make friends with people, but his appearance was so repellent that being part of a travelling exhibition was just about the only career option available to him.

The Grave Maurice is a uniquely named pub. Its odd name is derived from an anglicised corruption of the name of a Dutch Count, Graaf Maurits (1567–1725), who fought against the Spanish occupation of the Netherlands. It was a favourite drinking hole of the Kray brothers' gang. Another unusual name is that of the Blind Beggar pub at the junction with Cambridge Heath Road. Several explanations are put forward as

Star of David, Whitechapel Road.

to the derivation of this pub's name. Perhaps the most common of these is a reference to Henry, a son of the rebel Simon de Montfort whose force was defeated at the Battle of Evesham in 1265. Henry managed to escape in the guise of a blind beggar only to be taken in by a rich lady who later married him. This pub of course gained notoriety as the place where, in March 1966, Ronnie Kray shot and killed George Cornell, who was a rival gangster. He did so in front of witnesses, none of whom saw or heard anything!

Whitechapel Road becomes Mile End Road after the junction with Cambridge Heath Road. Outside No. 39 is a statue of Edward VII. This was erected in 1911 and was paid for by the local Jewish community. Rather oddly it features cherubs holding a book, a steamer, and a motor car. At Mile End Waste a bust and a statue of William Booth (1829–1912) may be seen. A fiery evangelist, in 1868 he held his first open air preaching meeting at this spot. Despite being pelted with verbal insults and more tangible physical missiles, Booth set up the London Revival Society and in 1878 this became the Salvation Army.

A welcome and charming respite from the bustle of the Mile End Road is provided by the Trinity Almshouses that were opened in 1695 by the Corporation of Trinity House. Their original purpose was to provide a hostel for twenty-eight 'decayed' masters or commanders of merchant ships and their relicts or widows. Much of the complex was destroyed by bombing in the Second World War but fortunately it was rebuilt in the same style. At the corner of Mile End Road and Cleveland Way, what was at first a small department store was opened in 1850 by Thomas Wickham. As business expanded, he needed more space and acquired a good site next door but one. However, try as he might, he could not persuade Mr Spiegelhalter, the shopkeeper of No. 81 (the intervening property), to sell up. Wickham's was rebuilt on a grand scale in the late 1920s but had to be built around No. 81. This rather spoilt the effect of the new store. Wickham's closed in 1969 and the building is now divided up into smaller units, but the cheeky little No. 81 survives as evidence that not every man has his price.

Pass Stepney Green tube station and just after the junction with Globe Road is a small arched entry called Mile End Close. Thousands must pass this entry daily and not notice it, but were they to pass through the arch they would find a delightful hidden piece of *rus in urbe*. Here are two rows of cottages whose front gardens when the authors last visited (April 2010) were a riot of flowers and greenery. There could be no greater contrast than that between the bedlam created by the traffic and the stark ugliness of the buildings along the Mile End Road and the bucolic tranquillity through that arch. Serendipity indeed!

Cross to the south side of Whitechapel Road and Mile End Road and walk to the junction with Stepney Green. Veer right into Hannibal Road and on the corner of Hannibal Road and Cressy Place is the flat, in Cressy Buildings, where the abortionist Vera Drake, played by Imelda Staunton, lived in the 2004 film of the same name. From Cressy Place, join Stepney Green where No. 37, Geere House, is a very handsome building erected in 1694 for a family that made its fortune from the East India Company. It is a reminder that Stepney at the time was a village far enough away from the smells, noise, overcrowding and dirt of the City to be fashionable. There are other

81 Mile End Road. Not every man has his price.

Mile End Close. Bucolic tranquillity amid urban bedlam.

fine old houses along Stepney Green.

On Stepney Green there is a quaint clock, commemorating the life and works of Stanley Bean Atkinson, a well-known local councillor. A drinking fountain erected in 1884 is close by. At the corner of Garden Street on the south side is a ruined Congregational church.

St Dunstan and All Saints' church in its sizeable churchyard looks out of place and more like a country church than a building in the heart of the East End. The church was probably founded in the tenth century, although only a Saxon rood stone remains of this church. The chancel dates from the thirteenth century and much of the rest is fabric rebuilt after fires and war damage. There is a legend that St Dunstan (909–988), while busy spreading the good word, moonlighted as a blacksmith and that one day he was banging away on his anvil when the Devil arrived at the forge in the guise of a beautiful young woman, determined to seduce him. She pirouetted around, ogling him, but as she did so her skirt rode up revealing the Devil's cloven hooves. Dunstan instantly sprang into action, taking up a pair of red-hot tongs and clamping them on the Devil's pert upturned little nose. With a scream of agony, the diabolical young beauty disappeared, probably in a puff of smoke. Mischievously, the authors wonder whether Dunstan's drastic action was motivated by frustration. He must have thought that he was on to an extremely good thing when this girl turned up unexpectedly at his forge, giving him the glad eye. Feeling his sap rising in eager anticipation, how seriously irked he would have been when the cloven hooves caught his eye.

Having looked at the church, readers might want to go into Ben Jonson Road off Stepney Green where at No. 58, Solent House, is a plaque to 'Doctor' Thomas John Barnardo (1845–1905). This was the site of his first hostel for parentless or homeless children. He never actually qualified as a doctor but that does not detract from the merit of the work he did in Britain and overseas. His motto was 'no destitute child ever turned away'.

Return to Mile End Road noting the impressive Dunstan House tenements built by the East End Dwelling Company on the west side of Stepney Green and a fine ghost advertisement on the frontage of No. 4. Both of these are best seen from the east side.

Proceed along the south side of Mile End Road and Sidney Street is on the left. This street gained immortality in London lore when it was the scene of a famous siege in January 1911. Police investigating the murder of three policemen during an attempted robbery in Houndsditch discovered a cell of East European anarchists using robbery to raise funds for political purposes. Acting on information received, they surrounded No. 100 Sidney Street, where a number of the gang were holed up. The police, supported by a contingent of Scots Guards, exchanged gunfire with the occupants but the siege was lifted when the building caught fire. Two bodies were recovered from the burnt-out building but a third gang-member thought to have been on the premises, the mysterious 'Peter the Painter', is believed to have got clean away. This was remarkable enough in itself but he did so to such effect that nothing official was ever heard of him again. Inevitably this has provoked speculation that he was never there, or that perhaps he was a government agent, or that there was something being hidden from the public about the whole affair. Winston Churchill, never averse to a good scrap,

Ghost advert,
Stepney Green.

was Home Secretary at the time and he attracted criticism for supervising operations himself and being unduly heavy-handed. Sidney Street now bears no resemblance to how it was a hundred years ago but at the far end of the street, close to Commercial Road, a block of flats named Siege House stands on the site of No. 100.

The Royal London Hospital is very prominent on the south side of Whitechapel Road. This was founded in 1740 in Bunhill Fields, closer to the City, but needed a larger site and moved here in 1757. It has grown into a not particularly attractive complex of buildings that have accumulated since that time. A plaque to Edith Cavell (1865–1915) can be seen. She trained and worked at the hospital and was later shot in Belgium by the Germans for aiding the escape of Allied servicemen. In the courtyard of the hospital is a huge statue of Queen Alexandra (1844–1925), the long-suffering wife of Edward VII. She was a notable patron of the hospital. A clump of carob trees can be seen. The carob, *Ceratonia siliqua*, is a member of the legume family and native to the

Mediterranean. It is distinctly uncommon in Britain. Behind the pub in Stepney Way is a pub with the unusual name of the Good Samaritan. It has a fine sign depicting a doctor.

Turn left at the junction with New Road and immediately left into Mount Terrace. Here is a terrace of old houses displaying a number of firemarks. Before public fire brigades developed well on in the nineteenth century, insurance companies ran their own fire brigades and they marked the premises they insured with distinctive badges incorporating their motif. This helped the brigade to identify which premises were on fire although it would have been just as simple to spot the one emitting flames, smoke and sparks. The badges or firemarks were usually made of lead or iron and, because of demolition, redevelopment, wear and tear or theft, they have become increasingly scarce. Those in Mount Terrace are not in very good condition but are at least still *in situ*. Mount Terrace takes its name from being on the site of fortifications thrown up by Parliamentary troops to defend London from attack by Royalist forces during the Civil War of the 1640s. It was a very noticeable small hill in otherwise flat terrain and became a place where children played. No trace of the mount survives except in two local street names.

At the junction of Whitechapel and Fieldgate Roads stands a remarkable survival. This is the Whitechapel Bell Foundry. This was established in Houndsditch in 1420 but it moved to its present site in 1738. It is actually Britain's oldest manufacturing company and a survivor of many of the small companies engaged in the metal trades that used to be such a feature of this district. In this rather understated foundry were cast bells that have rung out across the world, including the Liberty Bell of Philadelphia, cast in 1752, and the bell commonly known as Big Ben, which was made in 1858 and weighs well over thirteen tons. The foundry can be visited by arrangement.

A little further on towards the City stands Altab Ali Park. This was the yard of the former St Mary's church known as 'The Whitechapel' which gave the district its name. Altab Ali was a local Bangladeshi working man who was the victim of a racially motivated assault and murder.

Turn left into White Church Lane and left into Commercial Road. Cross and turn east to the junction with Hessel Street. This otherwise unexceptional street is named after Pheobe Hessel (1713–1821). Known as 'The Stepney Amazon', she was an extraordinary woman who served as an infantryman in the British army for seventeen years without her sex being revealed. She went on to die at the extremely honourable age of 108.

Turn left from Hessel Street into Burslem Street and then right into Cannon Street Road. Just after passing under the railway, turn right into Cable Street. This street derives its name from the ropeyards and ropewalks which were once a feature of this district. The British Union of Fascists (BUF) led by Sir Oswald Mosley (1896–1980) was a group of racists, xenophobes and admirers of Hitler's way of doing things. They encouraged their supporters, most of whom were violent young thugs with few prospects and even less brains, to intimidate and beat up Jews and other visible minorities for the alleged 'crime' of taking the jobs and housing that the fascist Blackshirts claimed rightfully belonged to the indigenous population. The BUF had developed among the East End's significant social deprivation, but the area also had a

Whitechapel Bell Foundry.

strong tradition of left-wing radicalism, similarly a product of inequality.

In October 1936 the BUF announced its intention of marching along Cable Street in large numbers deliberately to intimidate the substantial local population of Jews and other ethnic minorities. In the event, 3,000 BUF supporters turned out but much larger numbers of local people, Jews and anti-fascists, arrived, determined to prevent this provocation. Despite a huge police presence, the fascists were prevented from going any further by barricades at the junction of Cable Street and Leman Street. The day turned as much into an anti-police as an anti-fascist demonstration as the local people indiscriminately pelted fascists and police alike with brickbats, cobbles, refuse and any other missiles that came to hand. This was the famous 'Battle of Cable Street'.

Ensign Street is the next street along Cable Street going eastwards. Turn sharp left for Grace's Alley and Wilton's Music Hall. From the outside this provides an excellent imitation of a derelict building, which indeed it once was. It was originally the Prince of Denmark pub, but it was reopened as a music hall in 1859. It underwent many

Wilton's Music Hall.

vicissitudes before being scheduled for demolition in the 1960s, yet despite its outward appearance the show is most certainly still going on inside.

Return to Cable Street and turn immediate left into Dock Street, where immediately on the left can be seen a red plaque commemorating the Battle of Cable Street. Continue northwards from Dock Street into Leman Street, where Aldgate East tube awaits you. Alternatively, turn left at Whitechapel High Street and continue into Aldgate High Street; if refreshment is required, why not have a drink in the Hoop & Grapes? This is an ancient hostelry dating back to 1598. It somehow managed to survive the Great Fire of London in 1666 and now proudly boasts that it is the only surviving timber-framed building in the City, new buildings of this sort having been banned after the Fire. Note that this pub, as with so many others in the vicinity, is closed at weekends.

Before crossing to Aldgate tube, note the ward boundary markers on the wall just to the right of the pub's door.

3

Clerkenwell

Clerkenwell is slightly uphill from the City of London, and in ancient times it enjoyed the reputation of being comparatively healthy and well-watered, possessing many springs and the River Fleet in the west; this sizeable stream had a flow powerful enough to turn a number of watermills. Clerkenwell's position, away from the worst of the City's smells, noise and general squalor, attracted the interest of monastic orders. The earliest of these were the Benedictine nunnery of St Mary and the nearby Priory of the Knights of St John of Jerusalem, better known as the Knight's Hospitaller. They dated from around 1140, at which time the surrounding area was fertile agricultural land. Close by, but just outside the district and founded more than two centuries later, was the Carthusian establishment which became known as Charterhouse. The district derived its name from the Clerks' Well or *Fons Clericorum* at which the Company of Parish Clerks from the City annually acted out mystery plays.

These monasteries provided business and jobs and attracted some settlement around them, but they were suppressed and their assets seized in the Dissolution of the Monasteries in 1539–40. The land that they had previously owned and the buildings themselves could be obtained at bargain-basement prices and those with ready cash rushed to buy property which could only accumulate in value. The names or titles of some of these opportunists are recalled in such street names as Aylesbury and Albemarle. At one time the parcels of land they owned would have constituted spacious country estates surrounding opulent mansions.

The nature of the district began to change in the seventeenth century. Increasingly, Clerkenwell took on an industrial character. London was growing in national and world importance and Clerkenwell became an overspill suburb with the advantage for craft workers that it was outside the restrictive jurisdiction of the guilds of the City. So the district came to be characterised by small-scale but skilled industries sometimes introduced to this country by refugees who settled there to escape persecution on the Continent. Many of them were Huguenots. Examples of their trades were printing, the making of small but delicate metal instruments such as clocks and watches, and also jewellery-making. Somewhat later came brewing and distilling, attracted by the ample supplies of water. The population grew and the estates founded after the Dissolution tended to disappear under bricks and mortar. Clerkenwell took on a more diverse character. Some streets of houses for the well-to-do were built but elsewhere people often lived cheek-by-jowl with their places of employment. The proximity to Smithfield meat market meant that there were many cow-keepers whose byres added various smells and sounds to the heady mix of aromas and the growing hubbub that were beginning to characterise Clerkenwell.

In the eighteenth century, Clerkenwell developed into a place of resort because of its numerous wells and springs, to some of which therapeutic powers were ascribed. Londoners loved to stroll the short distance to the district and enjoy refreshments and entertainment at the various pleasure gardens that were on offer. The earliest of these resorts was Sadler's Wells, which opened in 1683. By the 1730s there were several others in competition, the best-known of which were probably the London Spa and the English Grotto. Fashion is capricious and the tendency was for a pleasure garden to open, become the place to which the modish crowds flocked, and then go into decline as the well-to-do became bored and moved on elsewhere when the clientele declined through the shabby genteel to the positively disreputable. The presence of the glitterati at these resorts was in marked contrast to what was happening close by. Rising crime in London put pressure on what then passed for a prison system, and Clerkenwell became the location of a number of penitentiaries; their presence in turn led to the building of the Middlesex Sessions House.

Nothing, seemingly, could stop the inexorable growth of London and the ceaseless spread of bricks and mortar. Areas that were once detached were now fully embraced in the continuously built-up area and, in so doing, some greatly changed their character. In that sense, Clerkenwell's problem was probably that of being rather too central. It became a kind of workshop for the City of London. While some of the old skilled industries remained, they were joined by a variety of 'sweated' trades characterised by low pay, low skills and poor working conditions. The housing of workers and their families was unsanitary and overcrowded. Industrialisation had its victims, but there were always those who fought back and Clerkenwell gained a reputation for political radicalism. Many meetings and marches started at Clerkenwell Green.

Clerkenwell also gained an unenviable reputation for overcrowded unsanitary criminal rookeries, the worst tending to be close to the banks of the River Fleet, which over the years turned from a limpid babbling brook into a stinking, festering receptacle for excrement (human and animal), offal, industrial effluent and all the general filth of this teeming, densely occupied quarter. The Fleet went by the alternative names of the 'Hole-bourne' (from which 'Holborn' of course derives), the River of Wells and Turnmill Brook. Progressively, from the eighteenth century, the Fleet was built over. Farringdon Road runs almost entirely along and over the course of the Fleet which is now only a storm sewer. Farringdon and Clerkenwell Roads and Rosebery Avenue were built in the late nineteenth century to relieve traffic congestion but also to drive a wedge through the area and help to destroy the appalling rookeries that were such a feature of this area.

From being a depressing inner-city district with a declining population, Clerkenwell has enjoyed a remarkable revival since the 1980s. Slums have been demolished, good older property has been renovated, the small manufacturing industries have largely gone and their premises have been given over to plush apartments or the offices of companies engaged in a variety of post-industrial activities.

For the purposes of this book, Clerkenwell will be taken as the area bounded by Turnmill Street, Cowcross Street, St John Street, Skinner Street, Rosebery Avenue and Clerkenwell Road.

The Walk

Leave Farringdon Underground station and cross the road. Look back at the station frontage. Farringdon was the terminus of the world's first underground railway. This ran from Paddington and was opened in 1863. The façade of the station is original and it still manages to look stylish. Note the full name which has not been used for over a hundred years.

Turn right along Cowcross Street. Opposite is the Castle pub. Note the sign of the three brass balls protruding from the front of the pub. The story is that the future George IV was out on the town one night when he was a young man. He often enjoyed an evening moving around incognito, drinking in various low taverns and pubs and gambling for high stakes. Even by the standards of British royalty, George was dissipated and it is typical of him that he was an avid but unsuccessful gambler. He was broke and about to ruefully make his way back home when he decided to pop into the Castle. He offered an expensive ring to the landlord. He was not recognised and the landlord was only too happy to give him a cash loan against the surety of the ring. The Prince happily went back to do some more gambling, albeit with no greater success. The next day he sent a servant to redeem the ring. He also sent him with a letter gratefully authorising the landlord to set himself up as a pawnbroker. Ever since that time, the Castle has been the only pub in Britain which is also a legal pawnbroker's business.

The name of Cowcross Street is an indication of the proximity of Smithfield Market. There was once a cross where Cowcross Street meets St John's Street, and animals would have passed this way literally in droves going to Smithfield. The nearby former Chicken Lane, Duck Lane and the still extant Cock Lane are also all reminders of the dominating local presence of Smithfield Market. On the right is a short street called Greenhill's Rents. John Greenhill owned much land in this area on which they erected buildings in 1735. They then let these out, hence the curious 'rents' part of the street name. There are other streets with similar names elsewhere in London.

At the junction with St John's Street, turn left and then left again into St John's Lane. Several buildings in St John's Street still display hoists, evidence of their former use as warehouses. Most of these are now apartments or what are euphemistically called

The Castle pub with its pawnbroker's three brass balls.

'workspaces'. On the left is Albion Place. Albion was a Roman name for the British Isles. In the eighteenth and nineteenth centuries, a burst of patriotic fervour led to many streets and pubs being given the name 'Albion'. On the right, a narrow entry is called Passing Alley. It used to be called 'Pissing Alley' but the name was bowdlerised in the nineteenth century because someone thought that people needed to be protected from such rudeness. It got its original name because that is precisely what people frequently did in it.

Facing is St John's Gate erected in 1504 when it became the main gateway to the important Priory of St John of Jerusalem which had been founded in the twelfth century. The monastic order of the Knights of St John of Jerusalem, otherwise known as the Knights Hospitallers, had been established to guard and provide accommodation

Passing Alley of yesteryear.

Passing Alley today.

for pilgrims travelling to sites in Palestine that were sacred to the Christian faith. Of this once major building only this gatehouse survives above ground, although there is an extremely fine crypt. The Priory was dissolved around 1539 and most of it was eventually demolished, but the gatehouse has remained as a notable landmark and has seen various uses. In the early eighteenth century it was a coffee house/tavern run by the father of the famous artist William Hogarth. The business failed. This is hardly surprising since the customers were required to speak only in Latin. Later on it housed a publishing company which produced the *Gentleman's Magazine*, numbering among its contributors Dr Johnson and Oliver Goldsmith. It went on to become a parish watch house and was again a pub for a time. In 1874 it was bought by the Order of St John of Jerusalem and in 1877 the St John Ambulance organisation was inaugurated there. A small museum can be visited.

St John's Gate today.
Opposite page: St John's Gate of yesteryear.

St. John's Gate from
Jerusalem Passage

Turn left into St John's Path for Britton Street. Immediately on the left of this street is the Jerusalem Tavern which is interesting because it has been a pub for less than twenty years and yet it very successfully attempts to provide the surroundings and ambience of just the kind of convivial tavern that Dr Johnson would have enjoyed.

Turn northwards along Britton Street and the impressive building which formerly housed the Middlesex Sessions House will be seen. This ceased to be used for its original purpose in 1919 and went through a variety of guises before being expensively restored to serve as a Masonic institution. The façade displays a number of sculptured reliefs symbolic of justice and mercy.

The Sessions House presides over Clerkenwell Green, which has very little greenery but is still recognisably a village centre and over the years has witnessed many meetings and demonstrations held in support of left-wing political ideas and activities. The Crown Tavern may have been patronised by Karl Marx and certainly served Vladimir Lenin, when they were both political exiles. No. 37 Clerkenwell Green is an unpretentious pedimented building opened in 1737 as a charity school for the children of poor Welsh Londoners. It went through various incarnations including a period when it housed the editorial offices of *Iskra*, a revolutionary socialist newspaper produced by Russian exiles. Lenin, the leader of the Bolshevik Revolution, worked here in 1902. The building now houses the Marx Memorial Library. This was established in the early 1930s as a response the burning of 'seditious' literature in Germany at the time.

Turn left into Clerkenwell Close. On the left is one of London's more eccentric pubs, the Three Kings. There is nothing corporate about the design of the name on the façade and London does not possess any other pub sign resembling that on display. (Unfortunately the oddball name sign was missing in April 2010 – only temporarily we hope). It was designed to celebrate the proud tradition of craftsmanship which has for so long been a feature of Clerkenwell. The windows, too, are worth looking at. Two of them advertise the former brewery of Mann, Crossman & Paulin, just one of the dozens of brewing firms in the greater London area whose names disappeared from the London streets in the twentieth century. Mann's was a large brewer but it was taken over by Watney's in the late 1950s. Few industries can equal brewing for evidence of aggressive corporate capitalism.

Across the road is the church of St James. This is built on the site of St Mary's nunnery. We do not normally enter buildings on these walks but this church is notable for its 'modesty boards', an odd and rare feature. These were placed along the stairs to prevent male worshippers feasting their eyes on the legs of women worshippers using the stairs. Although the women would have worn long skirts and very little leg would have been visible, men in those days could get quite worked up by even a fleeting glimpse of a female ankle. Externally, the church spire bears more than a passing and intentional resemblance to that of St-Martin-in-the-Fields.

Leave the church and turn left through the gate and walk to the far steps leading up to a bricked-up doorway. To the right of these steps is a very weathered headstone marking the burial place in 1834 of the tragic Ellen Sternberg and her four young children. They were stabbed to death by her husband, who then completed the rout of his family by stabbing himself to death. As was the way with suicides, he was buried elsewhere – at a crossroads although not, as some people have claimed, with a stake through his heart.

Return to Clerkenwell Close and turn right. Notice the almost overpowering tenements on the left. George Peabody (1795–1869) was an immensely wealthy American businessman who threw vast amounts of money at a variety of good causes in the USA and at the building of what would now be called 'affordable housing' for the working class in London. In fact, the rent for these severe and austere-looking blocks could only be afforded by tenants in regular employment in skilled or semi-skilled lines of work. With the facilities they offered, they were a vast improvement on the slum rookeries they replaced, and the presence of blocks of flats of this kind is often an indication that they were built on or close to the site of such slums. This is true of several blocks in Clerkenwell, here and on the other side of Farringdon Road. On the north side of Clerkenwell Close is the Horseshoe, an unsung survivor of the thousands of small and basic street-corner working-class pubs. Today's pub-owning companies are far more interested in larger-capacity higher-turnover outlets. Turn right from Clerkenwell Close into Sans Walk. This curious name is that of a nineteenth-century man who was prominent in local politics.

On the left, note the former Hugh Myddleton School. In 1870 Forster's Education Act introduced universal elementary education in England. Directly elected, secular boards were established to run the schools, far and away the biggest being the one for London. It embarked on a massive programme of school-building, mostly in the city's poorer districts. The schools they built were characteristically three storeys high and designed deliberately to dominate their surroundings, a sermon in brick and often terracotta on what were seen as the desirable values and attitudes that these schools were intended to inculcate in their proletarian pupils. This school was opened in 1892. Demographic change led to the school's closure. In keeping with the gentrification of the area, it underwent extensive renovation and emerged as expensive apartments with heavy security to keep undesirables out. This is ironic since the site used to have heavy security to keep undesirables in! It stands where a house of correction was built in 1616. Keeping a complicated history simple, it was rebuilt and extended several times and from 1845 to 1846 served for many years as the Middlesex House of Detention. It hit the headlines in 1867 when a cell of Fenians (Irish nationalists) tried to blow down the walls to release some comrades who were imprisoned inside. A spectacular explosion was detonated which blew a large hole in the prison wall. The force also blew down a block of houses opposite, causing several fatalities and many serious injuries. None of the prisoners escaped. One man, Michael Barratt, was found guilty in connection with this explosion and was hanged outside Newgate Prison in 1868, the last public hanging in Britain. Some of the cells of the old bridewell still exist under the former school and used to be part of a museum.

Sans Walk joins Woodbridge Street at its intersection with Sekforde Street. The modest but seemly and attractive streets in this area were built on land originally owned by Thomas Sekforde in the sixteenth century. The terraced buildings to be seen now mostly date from the 1820s, although some of the houses are newer replicas.

Peabody Buildings, Clerkenwell Close.

Where Woodbridge Street and Sekforde Street intersect a long blank wall is a reminder of the former presence of Nicholson's Distillery, one of several such businesses in the area. Apart from having a splendid heraldic sign, the Sekforde Arms also has a little reminder of brewing history. Set into the wall is a ceramic tile with a toby jug, the trade mark of Charrington & Co., another erstwhile London brewer.

Walk up Sekforde Street towards St John Street. On the left, notice the stuccoed frontage with the legend 'Finsbury Bank for Savings. Instituted AD 1816. Erected 1840.' Sekforde Street is good for aficionados of coal-hole covers. These are made of cast iron, nearly always circular and between 12 and 24 inches in diameter. They are often embossed with designs incorporating the maker's name and as such they are of interest to students of industrial history as they serve as reminders of London's long-lost but once numerous iron foundries. The purpose of the cover was to provide access via a chute to the coal cellars of 'superior' terraced houses. London used to have

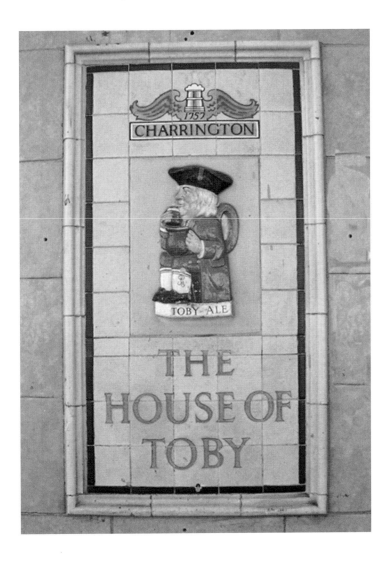

Toby trademark of the old Charrington Brewery, Sekforde Arms.

hundreds of thousands of such items of street furniture but their numbers have been decimated over the years.

At the junction with St John Street turn left into Skinner Street. On the left, the open space of Spa Fields recalls the district's therapeutic waters and former pleasure grounds. Rosoman Street is named after Thomas Rosoman, a speculative builder. Take a left turn into Exmouth Market. Note the date stone '1765' on the stuccoed front of 32/34. The north side was built later and the street renamed in honour of Admiral Edward Pellew, Lord Exmouth (1757–1833), a leading Royal Navy officer in the days of the 'Wooden Walls of England'. At the corner of Rosoman Street and Exmouth Market stands a building which was formerly the London Spa pub. This was a good historical name. It is now a Caribbean restaurant. Exmouth Market's character is changing out of all recognition. Gone is the merry banter of the Cockney costermongers and barrow-boys. The street has gone upmarket and is now a foodie's delight. It is lined with a cosmopolitan range of eating houses and the remaining stalls are given over to the selling of an eclectic selection of food from the four quarters of the planet. A blue plaque at No. 56 tells us that Joseph Grimaldi (1778–1837) lived there for several years, a member of the large Italian community which once characterised the district. Grimaldi became the clown that all the others wanted to be. In 1800 he was the first to wear the multi-coloured costume and to paint red half-moons on his cheeks. Also on the south side of Exmouth Market stands the church of the Holy Redeemer. Built in 1887–8 in a basilica style, this looks like an Italian church. Yet the architect was the thoroughly English John Spedding. Despite appearances and the former presence of so many Italians in the neighbourhood, this was always an Anglican establishment.

Cross at the junction of Farringdon Road and Rosebery Avenue and Cold Bath Square on the left. The eponymous Cold Bath was well noted for the coldness of its water. On the right is the massive Royal Mail Mount Pleasant depot built on the site of the Middlesex House of Correction which was in use from 1794 to 1886. Even by the standards of London prisons, Cold Bath Fields, as it was usually referred to, was a grim establishment. Its appalling regime had obviously come to the attention of the poet Samuel Taylor Coleridge who penned these lines:

> As he went through the Cold-Bath Fields he saw a solitary cell;
> And the Devil was pleased, for it gave him a hint
> For improving his prisons in Hell.

One street over on the left is Topham Street. This is named after Thomas Topham, a local strong man who, in 1741, lifted three hogsheads of water with a combined weight of 1,800 pounds. Among his other achievements were heaving his horse over a turnpike gate and lifting an oak table six feet long with his teeth. Continue down Rosebery Avenue – not the most inspiring of London's streets – and turn left into Laystall Street where at No. 10, under the shadow of some monumental tenements, there is an elaborate plaque to Guiseppe Mazzini (1805–1872), the Italian nationalist and democrat, who lived here for a time. Turn left into Clerkenwell Road. The Roman

Catholic church of St Peter is on the left, remaining evidence of the crowded Italian community that once occupied the neighbouring streets. St Peter's is the main church of Londoners of Italian origin and is based on a church of a similar basilica style in Rome. In the porch of St Peter's is a touching memorial to the victims of the *Arandora Star* tragedy. SS *Arandora Star* was a passenger liner launched in 1927 and owned by the Blue Star Line. In July 1940 she was carrying Italian and German internees from Liverpool to Canada. Most of them had lived in England for many years, in some cases for decades, and they presented no threat to the state. Many had made a fine contribution to British life. However, the government clearly thought that among their number there might be spies or saboteurs. Under the policy known pejoratively as 'collar the lot', they were regarded as enemy aliens, seized and put into custody. A total of 1,673 prisoners, guards, officers and crew were aboard when the *Arandora Star* was torpedoed by a German U-boat. Over 800 of them perished.

Memorial to the *Arandora Star* disaster, Clerkenwell Road.

Take a left turn into Herbal Hill. Its name, and those of Saffron Hill and Vine Hill nearby, recalls the fact that the soil hereabouts was noted for its fertility; fruit trees and a range of herbs were cultivated on land that later became built over as one of London's most festering slum rookeries. At the bottom of Herbal Hill note in Ray Street the Finsbury Borough boundary marker on the wall, just to the right of the Coach and Horses pub. The hilly nature of this quarter is due to it being built on the west side of the valley of the River Fleet. At one time the area was known as Hockley-in-the-Hole and was notorious for depravity and many of the barbaric activities previously associated with the Bankside district. It was also famed as a centre of the 'buttock-and-twang' enterprise. This simple criminal activity involved a woman, either pretending to be or actually a prostitute, luring an unsuspecting man into a dark corner for sex. As soon as he had largely immobilised himself by virtue of having his trousers around his ankles, her accomplice would emerge from the shadows and rob the punter at knifepoint, the victim being at a considerable disadvantage in this encounter.

From Ray Street cross Farringdon Road into Farringdon Lane. At 14/16 the Clerk's Well which gives the district its name is visible. The site of this well was lost for many years before being accidentally rediscovered in 1924 during building excavations. A window affords a view from the street and there is a display of information about it. Apparently the water is perfectly drinkable. From Farringdon Lane, return to Farringdon Underground station.

4

Part of the City

The City of London is a compact area, something more than a square mile, of enormous historical significance and interest. Chancery Lane stands at its western extremity, while in the east its furthest extent is Mansell Street at Aldgate and Middlesex Street. The Thames is its southern boundary and to the north it extends almost as far as Old Street.

London was founded by the Romans in the first century AD at the lowest feasible bridging point of the Thames. It became a highly sophisticated urban centre by the standards of the time. When the Romans departed, the City spent many decades in the doldrums but the establishment of St Paul's Cathedral in 604 marked a renewal of activity. The Normans placed their seat of government at Westminster, a short distance upstream, but built the formidable Tower of London to guard the City from external and also the internal threats posed by its volatile common people. In due course the City received various privileges of a commercial and financial nature, which made it a trading centre of world importance, and an autonomy that enabled certain of its citizens to accrue great wealth and power. Even the major setbacks of the Plague of 1665 and the Great Fire in 1666 – the former killing about one-fifth of the population and the latter destroying around seven-eighths of its buildings – could not quench the vitality of the City and the energy with which its leading citizens went about the business of enriching themselves.

The ruination of the City after the Great Fire prompted schemes for a grand rebuilding to replace the anarchic, overcrowded higgledy-piggledy arrangement that had perished in the fire. Sir Christopher Wren had ambitious plans for a rebuilt city of real grandeur, but vested interests provided insuperable opposition and the City quickly arose from the ashes, admittedly now with buildings of brick and stone rather than timber, but largely following its previous ancient street plan. However, the Great Fire irrevocably changed the nature of the City and a process of depopulation began which at first saw the wealthier inhabitants move westwards into desirable developing residential districts such as Mayfair and Marylebone. The City increasingly took on the character of a very successful commercial and financial centre, exemplified by the founding of the Bank of England in 1694. Further depopulation took place in the nineteenth century when new roads such as Queen Victoria Street were developed to cut swathes through and clear areas of slum housing whose populations drifted to growing inner-city suburbs such as Hackney, served by comprehensive electric tram routes.

Despite devastation from aerial bombing in the Second World War; the vicissitudes associated with economic booms and recessions; the emergence of a rival just down the road at Docklands; and a long-term relative decline in the UK's economic power; despite all this, the City arguably remains the world's major banking, insurance, commodities and foreign exchange centre. It is what it has been for centuries – a dynamic place unashamedly given over to making money.

This walk takes in some of the southern streets of the City, with their glaring juxtapositions of architectural style and scale, and begins and ends at Underground stations. It is easier to move about the City at weekends but then you miss most of the buzz and you may also have to go some way to find a pub that is open.

The Walk

We start at Blackfriars Underground station (closed for rebuilding at the time of writing in April 2010). Close by at 174 Queen Victoria Street is the Blackfriar pub. This is one of London's most eccentric but artistically significant pubs. Its eccentricity starts with its shape, which can only be likened to a wedge of cheese. Opened in 1875, it was remodelled at ground-floor level in the 1900s by a follower of the Arts and Crafts Movement loosely around a theme of 'Merrie England'. The interior contains a riot of variegated polished marble, alabaster figures and copper or bronze relief panels showing jolly-looking, rotund friars voicing pious statements often jocularly at odds with their own appearance or activities. Some of the reliefs are the work of a sculptor of national repute, Henry Poole RA. Outside, above the main door, the pub sign is the carved figure of an extremely stout, benevolent-looking friar. There are also various external bas-relief carvings and mosaics. Altogether it's a wonderfully zany pub and well worth a visit.

Much of the land in the vicinity was once occupied by the large Dominican monastery of Blackfriars which was dissolved in the late 1530s. Cross Queen Victoria Street and walk up to Blackfriars Lane and into a maze of narrow alleys and streets largely unchanged in disposition for hundreds of years. Turn right into Playhouse Yard where, in Ireland Yard, a fragment of the friary wall can be seen in the remnant of the churchyard of the former church of St Anne. Return to Blackfriars Lane and turn right. On the right note the coat of arms over the door of the Apothecaries Hall. Go right into Carter Lane where a City of London plaque acknowledges the site of the Blackfriars. Easily missed off Carter Lane is Church Entry. Here is one of those serendipitous discoveries. It is a tiny green open space probably unknown to 99.9

Fragment of the wall of the former Blackfriars monastery in Ireland Yard.

per cent of those who have lived all their lives in London. It stands where part of the nave of the Blackfriars stood. A quaint nameplate on the former St Ann's Vestry Hall in Church Entry indicates the presence on the premises not only of the Ancient Monuments Society but also a worthy body called the Friends of Friendless Churches, surely something of an oxymoron.

At the junction of St Andrew's Hill and Carter Lane note the parish boundary plate above L'Express. It says 'Farringdon Ward Without 1878'. Another marker is affixed to the building on the opposite corner. At the bottom of St Andrew's Hill is the church of St Andrew by the Wardrobe. This gained its strange name from being close to the Crown Wardrobe, where the accoutrements used by royalty for formal occasions were kept. Return to Carter Lane. Wardrobe Place is an easily missed entry on the right where some difficult-to-decipher ghostly lettering alludes to a long-forgotten business carried on there. Go back to Carter Lane and take a right into Addle Hill and then left into Knightrider Street. This odd name may or may not be a reference to it being part of the route along which knights from the Tower of London and Baynards Castle (which was close by) rode while on their way to jousts and similar frolics in the Smithfield district. At the end is a venerable pub known to many generations as The Horn but renamed as the Centre Page in recent years. The authors have no objection to its new name as such. It is certainly far better than the banal, even idiotic names so

Firefighters Memorial, St Peter's Hill.

frequently dreamed up by callow philistines at the pub-owning companies when they want to rebrand some harmless old hostelry. It may have appropriate historical roots but we do question the need for the change of name in the first place.

Turn left from Knightrider Street into St Peter's Hill. Here a powerful work in bronze called 'Blitz' commemorates the total of 1,002 UK firefighters who lost their lives while on duty in the Second World War. The authors like to see monuments to such unsung heroes rather than to the so-called great and good about whom myths have so often been woven for the self-serving purposes of history.

Standing boldly at the west front of St Paul's Cathedral is a statue of Queen Anne (reigned 1702–1714). This is a replica of one originally erected in 1712. The figure looks robust enough but really Anne did not have a particularly good life. By the time she was in her thirties she was worn out by continuous confinements. There were seventeen of these and all her progeny died young or stillborn. She gained some comfort from eating and drinking, both in excess. She became extremely corpulent and earned the affectionate nickname of 'Brandy Nan'. She suffered from severe gout and from convulsions; by the time she ascended the throne, she was a virtual invalid living in constant pain. When she died, her body was so swollen it had to be buried in a huge square coffin.

Note the polished granite bollards scattered around St Paul's Churchyard. These have to be among the poshest bollards in the metropolis. A comparative newcomer to the north side of St Paul's Churchyard is the Temple Bar. This contrives to look a trifle embarrassed as well it might since it dates back to the 1670s but has only been in its present position since 2004. Traditionally, Temple Bar stood at the point where Fleet Street became the Strand and it marked the westernmost limit of the City. The building to be seen today was a replacement for an earlier bar and was designed by Sir Christopher Wren. It played a prominent role in London folklore as it used to be a place for the display on tall spikes of the heads of executed traitors. These were supposed to act as a deterrent to the crime of treason but they became a popular attraction and many Londoners would stroll out on a Sunday afternoon to view these heads and then, if they wanted more, to proceed to Old London Bridge, which was frequently adorned with many other similarly severed heads. The seasoned voyeur would take a telescope with him for a close-up; otherwise a spyglass could be hired for a halfpenny. All good things have to come to an end – changing mores decreed that the practice of displaying the heads was barbaric. Many years later it was decreed that Temple Bar had to go because it was becoming a traffic obstacle. It was carefully dismantled in 1878 and re-erected at Theobalds Park in Hertfordshire, where it eventually became neglected and ruinous. However, its historical significance won it many friends and eventually it was once again dismantled and re-erected to form part of the Paternoster Square redevelopment. Hopefully its peripatetic days are over. Further on, note St Faith's Pump behind a set of railings. This was associated with the parish church of St Faith which had stood so close to the east end of St Paul's that it was demolished during extensions to that building.

By St Paul's tube station note the relief of the Panyer Boy. Panyers were baskets used for carrying bread; they were made hereabouts and bought by the bakers of nearby

Granite bollards, St Paul's Churchyard.

The Panyer Boy.

Bread Street. The plaque shows a nude boy sitting, possibly rather uncomfortably, on a panier. This stone was re-erected in 1964 and remembers an inn called the Panyer Boy, on or near the site, which was destroyed in the Great Fire. It also bears an inscription:

> When ye have sought the City round
> Yet still this is the highest ground.

Actually it isn't, because Cornhill is slightly higher. Cross into St Martin's Le Grand and a little further on the left is Postman's Park. It gained its odd name from being a place of relaxation for the postal workers at the nearby General Post Office. Hidden away in this little-known area of greenery is a display of tiles commemorating the heroism of ordinary men and women from the London area who unselfishly and heroically gave up their lives to save others, very often compete strangers. In St Martin le Grand stands one of the few remaining blue police call boxes. There were in effect mini police stations with a beacon on the top which flashed when HQ was trying to get in touch with officers out on patrol, Modern communications systems have rendered these boxes redundant. This box is a smaller model than the more commodious Tardis, made immortal in the *Doctor Who* television series.

Return down St Martins le Grand and turn left into Cheapside. In medieval times, this was the main marketplace of London. At the junction with Wood Street on the north side is a tiny shop so much older and smaller than the temples of Mammon all around. There is also a large plane tree. The tree marks the site of the church of St Peter in Chepe, destroyed in the Great Fire. The tree may not be damaged nor may any building be put up that affects it in any way while it is still alive.

On the south side at the junction with Bow Lane is the church of St Mary-le-Bow. This has a splendid gilded dragon for a weathervane, a tower with an unusual door and an open balcony. In 1331 a wooden balcony had been erected so the Queen and her attendants could watch a joust. This balcony collapsed, precipitating the ladies to the street below and injuring many of them. After this it was decided to make the balcony that can now be seen. This church is of course famous for the old legend that for a person to claim themselves as a Cockney, they had to be born within the sound of Bow Bells. In earlier times the sound of the bells would have carried much further than they do now given the permanent hubbub of the metropolis. In 1196, during the reign of Richard I, the church found itself the centre of attention when it was the scene of a protest by William Fitzosbert. Little is known about him except that he was wealthy and he had fought with distinction in the Crusades. He was a strong and powerfully built man with a commanding presence. He was also a spellbinding demagogue. Fitzosbert was a natural rebel, nicknamed 'Longbeard' because he sported an enormous facial appendage purely to bate the Norman rulers, who were mostly clean-shaven. Hugely popular with the common people of London but a running ulcer as far as the authorities were concerned, he frequently held forth about the iniquitous burden of taxation on the ordinary folk and the decadence of the clergy and the various unjustified privileges they enjoyed. The authorities decided to move against him and they sent a force of soldiers to apprehend him. He killed one of them and then took refuge in the church tower, apparently already supplied with food and arms and two mistresses in case boredom set in. It was decided to smoke him out and after considerable damage had been done to the church he had to rush into the street for fresh air. He was seized, thrown into a gloomy and fetid dungeon and was later executed at Smithfield, perhaps the first of the many poor wretches to die there. Some regard him as a people's hero. One historian, however, described him as a 'filthy fornicator' and a 'polluter of concubines'.

From the south side of Cheapside turn down Bow Lane. On the right is Groveland Court and Williamson's Tavern. At the end of this alley can be seen a pair of wrought-iron gates. These were presented by William III and Mary II to the Lord Mayor who then lived in the building. Turn left into Watling Street. By the north wall of the church of St Mary Aldermary is a charming sculpture called 'The Cordwainer'. Originally, a cordwainer was a worker using Cordovan Spanish leather to make shoes.

The Cordwainer,
Watling Street.

Later, cordwainers made many other articles, such as bottles, from leather. There were formerly many leather workers in this part of the City. The church has its strange name because at one time there were nineteen churches in London with the name of St Mary's. The 'Alder' element in the name means this one is the oldest. We do not often venture inside buildings on these walks but make an exception in this case because on the north wall near the altar is a memorial tablet which is completely blank. Various theories are put forward to explain this quirk. One of these claims that a widow had had the clearly expensive memorial erected in fond memory of her recently deceased first husband when she fell passionately in love with another man. In her new state of sublime happiness, she either forgot to have the memorial completed or, in her fickleness, decided that he was past history and not worth spending the money on.

Go to Mansion House tube at bottom end of Bow Lane. Continue into Garlick Hill, which was the place where garlic was sold in medieval times (always useful for

Memorial at the church of St John the Baptist, Cloak Lane.

smothering the taste of rancid meat), and then take a left into Great St Thomas Apostle and Cloak Lane. There is a memorial on the north side of Cloak Lane. This records that when the District Railway was built in 1884 it was necessary to disturb the human remains interred in the graveyard attached to the church of St John the Baptist upon Walbrook. This memorial states that these remains were respectfully moved to a vault just below. Since the District and Circle Lines run just a few feet below, they are unlikely to get much rest. Walk left into College Hill. The church of St Michael Paternoster Royal is a much remodelled building of medieval origin but initially rebuilt by Wren. It contains the Mission for Seafarers. Turn left into College Street where the main door of Innholder's Hall has superb carving supposedly by the hand of Grinling Gibbons. Opposite is a boundary marker.

Go left at Dowgate Hill to Cannon Street and the London Stone. This is set into the wall of No. 111, Cannon Street but it was previously on the south side of the street in the

Decorative house
number, Laurence
Pountney Hill.

wall of St Swithin's church. It is a fairly undistinguished piece of Clipsham limestone
from Rutland and no one really knows its history although it received its first mention
in 1198. It is sadly neglected. A little further up St Swithin's Lane, on the west side, is
a fine hanging advertisement showing the silhouette of a Spanish man. The product
being advertised is Sandeman's sherry. Return to and continue east along Cannon
Street. In Abchurch Yard a ghost street name can be seen. Next, cross Cannon Street to
Laurence Pountney Hill on the south side. Here there are cherubs in a shell doorway
and a nicely polished numeral at the portal of No. 6. Laurence Pountney Hill takes
its strange name from that of a church destroyed in the Great Fire and never rebuilt.
Return to Cannon Street and turn right into Martin Lane where the Old Wine Shades
can be seen. This establishment seems to be weighted down by its own antiquity and
claims to be the oldest wine house in the City. At least part of the building survived the
Great Fire and what can be seen now is a rebuilding on the same site.

Timber from Roman
jetty, Church of St
Magnus the Martyr,
Lower Thames
Street.

From Monument tube station walk down Fish Street Hill. This was once the main
approach from the City to the old London Bridge. The Monument was designed to be
not only a memorial but also a telescope and test bed for various intended experiments.
It was built, quite slowly it has to be said, between 1671 and 1677 to commemorate
the Great Fire of 1666. It is a fluted Doric column 202 feet high, this being the exact
distance from the house in Pudding Lane where the conflagration started. As might
be expected, scapegoats were sought for this appalling catastrophe. At the time the
Monument was erected, England was in the throes of heightened religious hatred and
intolerance. Rumours abounded of an international plot masterminded by the Pope
to restore Roman Catholicism to the position of dominance it had enjoyed before
the English Reformation. It was believed that the Catholics would stop at nothing to
achieve their aims. Evidence of this mass hysteria was an inscription on the pedestal
of the Monument that accused the 'Popish faction' of starting the fire. Removed and
then replaced on a couple of occasions, this example of official bigotry was finally
excised in 1831 (it now rests in the Museum of London). A by-law rather oddly forbids
anyone to beat a carpet against the base of the Monument.

Grasshopper sign of the former Martins
Bank, Lombard Street.

The church of St Magnus the Martyr stands on the south side of Lower Thames
Street and was located at the northern foot of the old London Bridge. In what is left of
its yard can be seen some stones from the old bridge and a piece of timber found in
Fish Street Hill in 1921 and thought to have come from a wharf on the Thames built in
the time of the Romans.

Return north into Eastcheap. On the north side at Nos 23–5, near the junction with
Philpot Lane, can be descried some small carved mice. When the men were erecting this
building, they became fond of some quick-witted mice that learned to make the most
of their generosity and wax fat on tasty titbits. Nos 33–35 somehow seem out of place
with their riot of frivolous gothic gables and arches. Continue into Lombard Street.
This is notable for the survival of a number of attractive signs relating to erstwhile
banks that had their premises here. They include a very handsome grasshopper
projecting from No. 68, the trademark of the former Martins Bank, the headquarters of
which were in Liverpool.

Between Lombard Street and Cornhill, on the former's north side, there is an
unexpected labyrinth of small passages, including Change Yard which is particularly

THE CORPORATION OF

ON THIS SITE BETWEEN 1680 AND 1778 STOOD JONATHAN'S COFFEE HOUSE, THE PRINCIPAL MEETING PLACE OF THE CITY'S STOCKBROKERS

THE CITY OF LONDON

Plaque marking the site of the former Jonathan's Coffee House, Change Alley.

confusing because it has no fewer than four entrances. There are two plaques in Change Alley referring to the sites of early coffee houses. Among the ancient hostelries hidden away in this backwater is the George and Vulture pub in George Yard, Simpson's Chop House in Birchin Lane, and the Jamaica Wine House in St Michael's Alley, a pub on the site of the first coffee house in London, started in 1652 by a man of Mediterranean origin called Pasqua Rosee. St Peter's church has a gate with rather fine image in iron of St Peter holding his keys aloft. Try as they might, the authors could not descry the devils looking down on the church from the nearby buildings, the result of a difference of opinion between the developers and the church.

Back in Cornhill, at No. 39, there is a private plaque which informs anyone who notices it that Thomas Grey (1716–1771) lived there. In such a hub of the world of finance, while it might just about be possible to think of the curfew tolling the knell of parting day, the idea of the lowing herd winding slowly o'er the lea distinctly lacks resonance.

Gateway to St Olave's church, or 'St Ghastly Grim' as Dickens had it.

Continue from Cornhill into Leadenhall Street. Turn right into Billiter Street. Go to the junction with Fenchurch Street and cross into Mark Lane. Take a left at Hart Street. St Olave's church is mentioned in *The Uncommercial Traveller* by Dickens under the guise of 'St Ghastly Grim'. This is on account of the very curious late seventeenth-century gateway adorned, if that is the right word, with gruesome *memento mori* in the form of death's heads and crossbones. It is capped with lethal-looking spikes.

Continue into Crutched Friars where, on the right, The Ship has an interesting frontage. Walk along Crutched Friars. This delightfully named street refers to a long-gone friary in the vicinity. It belonged to the Friars of the Holy Cross, a mendicant order whose brethren wore a distinctive cross on their habits. A pub called the Crutched Friars stands in this street and at one time sported a sign that mistakenly showed a couple of friars hobbling along on crutches. This may have been a deliberate mistake for fun. Close by on the left is one of London's oddest street names. This is French Ordinary Court. Its origin is perhaps not quite as exotic as might be expected. An 'ordinary' was a cheap restaurant usually with a fixed menu. One of these, standing in the vicinity and noted for the French flavour of its menu, was burned down in the Great Fire.

Continue along Jewry Street to the junction with Aldgate. Close by at the junction of Aldgate and Leadenhall Street stands Aldgate Pump. The original pump was a short distance away and seems to have received its first mention in the early twelfth century. The pump to be seen today was put up in 1871 and shows a rather fine spout of brass in the form of a dog's head. An old expression was 'a draught (draft) on Aldgate Pump' which meant a cheque that was useless because there were no funds to support it. Complete the walk by continuing to Aldgate and its tube station.

5

St James's and Mayfair

The 'West End' is a little difficult to define but few would dispute that this walk takes in a part of it. The area covered here is bounded by Haymarket, Piccadilly, Old Bond Street, New Bond Street, a very short stretch of Oxford Street, Davies Street, Charles Street, Shepherd Market, Piccadilly, St James's Street, Pall Mall and back to Haymarket. This area consists of parts of London where the ultra-rich and therefore powerful have lived, played, gambled, swindled each other, engaged in clandestine affairs and spent money conspicuously. They continue to do so.

The historical nature of this district means that the walker will pass innumerable commemorative plaques. Only a few, thought to be of particular interest, will be mentioned.

The Walk

From Charing Cross tube station, pass through Trafalgar Square and along Pall Mall East to Haymarket. As its name suggests, there was once a market for hay and straw here, largely to meet the demands of the rich 'carriage folk' who resided in the vicinity. For a period in the nineteenth century, Haymarket was a notorious centre for prostitution: harlots of every age, size, race and speciality touted their wares in a brazen fashion. They included children aged ten and younger. One visitor described the Haymarket as 'the centre of the surging mass of nocturnal corruption'. Although by this time it was witnessing less prostitution, the raffish nature of the Haymarket is alluded to by a gentleman in his diary dated 2 June 1859:

> I walked home at about 4am; broad daylight. The street scenes at that hour, especially at the top of the Haymarket, were quite Hogarthian. The last stragglers were just reeling out of the Piccadilly (a supper house) and talking and squabbling outside: two gentlemen in

evening dress, a few unwashed foreigners, several half-drunken prostitutes, one of whom, reeling away, drops her splendid white bonnet in the gutter, and another dances across the street, showing her legs above the knee: languid waiters in shirt sleeves stand looking on from their doors; two or three cabmen doze on the box behind their dozing horses: and a ragged beggarwoman skulks along in the shadow of the houses...

Haymarket today is still a place of entertainment and leisure with many coffee bars, eating houses and theatres: it rarely goes to sleep. In Orange Street, on the east side of Haymarket, a tablet inscribed 'James Street 1673' can be seen high up on the south side. This was the former name of the street. It is thought to be the second oldest street sign in London. On the north side of Orange Street is a Congregational church founded in 1693. It was originally established as a place of worship for Huguenot refugees. It passed into the control of the Church of England in 1776. Among its incumbents was the Revd Augustus Toplady. He is best known for being the author of the hymn 'Rock of Ages'. He deserves to be better known for stating, in all seriousness, that by the time he or she had reached the age of thirty, each human being had committed 630,720,000 sins. Unfortunately he never revealed the factual evidence on which this remarkable figure was based. He died of consumption in 1778 at the age of thirty-eight but not before, despite being severely debilitated, he had insisted on being carried into the church to preach an inflammatory sermon which refuted rumours that he had had second thoughts about his well-known and lifelong hatred of John Wesley.

Return to Haymarket. Only one old building survives. This is No. 34 which for many years was Fribourg & Treyer's tobacco shop. It has perhaps the best early eighteenth-century shopfront in London. It is now a gift shop.

Cross Piccadilly Circus, passing Eros on your right. This is officially known as the Shaftesbury Memorial Fountain. It was intended to commemorate the 7th Earl of Shaftesbury and his philanthropic works, but the figure with which it is topped turned out to be Eros the God of Love rather than the intended Angel of Christian Charity. It is regularly boarded up on occasions such as New Year's Eve when its gushing cascades might prove too much of a temptation to drunken revellers. Cross Piccadilly and walk along its north side. Sackville Street is notable for being the longest street in London without a turning off it. Burlington Arcade is a famous example of an early covered shopping mall. Oddly, it was built about 1820 by the owner of nearby Burlington House to stop the oafs and the oiks of the day from lobbing all kinds of rubbish over his garden wall. High above the Piccadilly entrance are the arms of the Chesham Family. These were placed there in 1911 at which time the Cheshams owned the arcade. Beadles, always ex-servicemen of peerless probity, are on duty to ensure that the rules of the arcade are observed at all times. It is forbidden to whistle or sing, brandish an opened umbrella, carry a large parcel, propel a perambulator or run. Few people ever do any of these twice. Although the offence may not be specifically referred to, woe betide any uncouth youth who tries to skateboard through the arcade which, at 585 feet, is the longest in the UK. It is lined with small, upmarket shops.

From Piccadilly turn right into Old Bond Street which soon becomes New Bond Street. In Stafford Street on the west side of Old Bond Street, the Goat pub advertises its presence with a full-sized model goat protruding from the frontage. Close to where Old Bond Street runs into New Bond Street is a street sculpture showing life-size figures of Winston Churchill and Franklin D. Roosevelt. It is called 'Allies'. Perhaps it should also have included Josef Stalin because the three ill-assorted bedfellows of the UK, USA and USSR were responsible between them for agreeing on how the post-war planet should be carved up.

Most of the buildings in Bond Street date from the eighteenth century. It has always been a place for expensive and fashionable retail premises. It is the exclusiveness of this street which probably explains why it has never been extensively redeveloped. It remains narrow, the buildings and the businesses small-scale. Nos 165–9 display fine Victorian shopfronts. This is Asprey & Garrard, jewellers. Note the elegant barley twist columns. No. 26 is Tessier's goldsmiths. Tiffany & Co. at No. 25 has a fine arcaded

'Allies', Roosevelt and Churchill, Bond Street.

shopfront of black serpentine. Over Sotheby's at Nos 34–35 can be seen an ancient Egyptian sculpture of the goddess Sekhet that is estimated to be around 2,500 years old. It is perhaps the most bizarre shop sign in London and draws attention to the priceless antiquities and *objets d'art* sold there. It is thought to be the oldest outdoor sculpture in London. Numerous other shopfronts are worth a second look.

Among the tributaries on the west side of Bond Street is Bruton Street off which is Bruton Place. This L-shaped street provided stabling and coach houses for the owners of the grand mansions in nearby Bruton Street and Berkeley Square. The buildings are small-scale and Nos 36 and 38 still display the hoists used for shifting bags of provender. The Guinea is a noted pub, often referred to as 'The One Pound One'. The fame of its steak and kidney pies extends way beyond Mayfair, the district in which it stands. The name 'Mayfair' is a reference to a popular fair which used to be held annually in May in the vicinity of what is now Shepherd Market until it was suppressed in the mid-eighteenth century. The area was being developed with high-class residential property and those moving into the district did disliked the rowdiness and bawdy behaviour associated with the fair. It was for the same reason that public hangings ceased in 1783 at Tyburn, close to what is now Marble Arch.

Continue along New Bond Street. On the left Avery Row and Lancashire Court are surprising small-scale backwaters. Brook Street crosses New Bond Street. At Nos 23 and 25 on the south side of Brook Street, west of New Bond Street, are two blue plaques in piquant juxtaposition. No. 23 was the residence of the American rock star Jimi Hendrix from 1968 to 1969. Next door the plaque explains that this was where the German composer Handel lived and died. The proposal to erect the memorial to Hendrix next to that of Handel provoked furious opposition in some circles at the time.

Continue along New Bond Street and turn left into Oxford Street. This has a long history as a major route out of London for places to the west and south-west. It has had a variety of names in the past but Oxford Street seems to have become its established title when much of the land along its north side was bought by Edward Harley, Earl of Oxford, in 1713. Until the eighteenth century, it was a rustic lane leading through fields and plagued by footpads. In the late nineteenth century, it began to assume the character it has had ever since – that of a centre of retailing. It became an elongated high street largely with the kind of shops to be found in any high street in the UK except that many of Oxford Street's are larger. Another difference is the multitude of foreign tourists and the numerous small shops selling trashy gimcrack 'souvenirs'.

Turn left into Davies Street. This was developed from the 1720s but few of its buildings date from before the twentieth century. No. 53 on the west side is an attractive stuccoed building housing the administrative functions of the well-heeled Grosvenor Estate which owns much property here and elsewhere. At No. 58 is a large antiques emporium worth visiting because through it flows the Tyburn River. What can be seen is a small stream but it used to have a stronger flow. The river carved a slight valley out for itself, and the depression made by this can be seen as a dip in Oxford Street, Brook Street, Grosvenor Street and Piccadilly. The exterior of the antiques emporium shows a fine terracotta tiled sign for the Grosvenor Works, a former occupant.

The Grovesnor Works were former occupants of 58 Davies Street.

Continue along Davies Street to Berkeley Square. Many of its buildings are modern and obtrusive but on the west are some fine old houses dating from the mid-eighteenth century. No. 50 has been at the centre of rumour and counter-rumour for well over a hundred years. It is now occupied by an old-established firm dealing in antiquarian books, but for many years it was unoccupied because it was believed to be haunted. Various unexplained noises were heard by neighbours at times when the house was known to be empty and some said that a gang of coiners were surreptitiously using the house and circulating stories about ghosts in order to deter anyone from investigating. Phantoms come in varying degrees of scariness but whatever it was at No. 50 it definitely ticked the spooky box. Some said that the spectre was that of a child, starved to death in a locked upper room and seeking vengeance for the tribulations it had suffered. Another phantom was supposed to be that of a young serving girl who lived in the house and jumped out of the window to her death rather than succumb to the lecherous designs of her master. A third story is that of two penniless and benighted mariners in London one freezing winter's evening. They broke in, knowing nothing of the house's sinister reputation. They were composing themselves for sleep in an upper room when 'something' gruesome and menacing disturbed them so badly that one of them died from an instant heart attack. The other leapt from the window and impaled himself on the railings. He lived, but either could not or would not describe what he had seen. However, since the premises have been used for commercial purposes, no supernatural phenomena seem to have occurred. This does not prevent significant numbers of people from hanging around outside hoping or not hoping to see something. Incidentally, no nightingale has been known to sing in Berkeley Square.

Among the earliest residents of Berkeley Square was Ermengarde Melusina von der Schulenberg. George I had many mistresses but she was in the premier league. The King clearly thought that without her and another Hanoverian harlot by the name of Countess van Platen, life in dreary England would be quite insufferable and so he had them shipped over soon after he arrived, rather unwillingly, in this country. Now everyone knew that the enjoyment of mistresses was a harmless peccadillo resorted to by most kings, but to keep up their street credibility they normally equipped themselves with good-looking ones. In this respect, these two let the side down. The first, who was given the title of Duchess of Kendal, was grotesquely skeletal and the other, bestowed merely with the title of Countess of Darlington, was about as wide as she was tall. They quickly acquired the mocking nicknames of the 'Maypole' and the 'Elephant and Castle' and were the source of much ribald and frequently salacious comment. It is interesting to note that they were mocked mercilessly in a way that would simply not be regarded as acceptable in the supposedly more democratic twenty-first century.

Some of the block of old buildings of which No. 50 is one display very fine ironwork on their street frontages. They include cast-iron railings and wrought-iron lamp-holders and snuffers or extinguishers. Before the days of street lighting, those who could afford to would hire a link-boy to light them on their way home. He would carry a flaming torch dipped in pitch which he would extinguish at the outsize snuffers of the sort that can be seen here.

Leaving the south-east corner of Berkeley Square, walk into Berkeley Street. On the left is Hay Hill. When the future George IV was merely the Prince of Wales, on one occasion in the late 1790s he and his equally dissolute chums had been enjoying the salacious pleasures available in a brothel in Berkeley Street. They were making their way homewards when they were set upon by a gang of footpads and relieved of all the money they had. This amounted to just half-a-crown or twenty-five pence. The robbery took place in Hay Hill. On the right of Berkeley Street is Lansdowne Row. Note the sunken passage with bars at one end. Back in the eighteenth century, this passage was once used by a highwayman to effect an escape and the authorities decided to prevent a repetition by fixing the bars at one end.

Turn right into Fitzmaurice Place and left into Charles Street where there are a few buildings largely unchanged from the period in which they were built, around the 1740s. Some still show their original iron lamp-holders and stone obelisks in front of

Snuffer in Berkeley Square.

Decorative ironwork in Berkeley Square.

the doorways. At No. 22 a privately-sponsored plaque records that the Duke of Clarence (1765–1837) lived there briefly, a few years before he became king in 1830. His reign as William IV was a short and not particularly notable one. His father had sent him into the Royal Navy at the age of fourteen with instructions that no allowance was to be made for his social position. Nevertheless, he was promoted to rear-admiral at the age of twenty-four, the usual criteria of seniority and sometimes of merit not being applied in his case. His naval career earned him the nickname 'The Sailor King'. His other nickname was 'Silly Billy'. Above the front door of No. 36 is worn carved head of a gentleman wearing a laurel wreath. Who was he?

At the junction of Charles Street with Hay's Mews stands the Running Footman pub. This name is unique and refers to the former practice whereby rich 'carriage folk' would employ fit young men dressed in the family's livery to run ahead of their coach to ask publicans to make hospitality ready for their prestigious guests. They also often paid the tolls required for passing along turnpike roads. Many of these carriage folk lived in Mayfair.

Turn south from Charles Street into Chesterfield Street. And cross Curzon Street into Shepherd Market. You are now in a maze of narrow streets, alleys and buildings on a humble scale quite unlike many of the huge buildings previously passed on this walk. Shepherd Market is one of London's hidden urban villages and takes its name from the builder who laid it out around 1735. This is the site of the old May Fair. A privately erected plaque at 17 Trebeck Street claims to be on the site of the May Fair. The authorities probably found that the only way effectively to render extinct the fair and its undesirably boisterous behaviour was to build on the land where it took place. Shepherd Market unquestionably exudes the atmosphere of a village and is a lively, bustling spot with small shops, pubs and eating places.

From Shepherd Market move on to Hertford street and turn left into Down Street. On the west side shortly before the junction with Piccadilly is the unmistakeable ox-blood-coloured tiled frontage of the street-level London Underground station buildings designed by Leslie Green. They were opened in 1907 on what was then the Great Northern Piccadilly and Brompton tube. It was tucked away in an obscure and largely residential street whose affluent inhabitants made little use of public transport. It was also too close to Dover Street (now Green Park) and Hyde Park Corner tube stations and it never attracted much traffic. As early as 1909 some trains were scheduled to pass through without stopping. Down Street closed to passengers in May 1932 but was used by various highly secretive government agencies during the Second World War.

Turn left from Down Street into Piccadilly. This peculiar street name has excited curiosity for centuries. It is likely that it owes its quirky name to one Robert Baker, a country lad who came to London in the early seventeenth century to make his fortune and, unlike so many others, succeeded. He became a very successful tailor known especially for the 'piccadillies' or 'picadils' he made, these being a decorative frill around collars and cuffs. He made enough money to become a land developer and started his enterprise around the east end of what is now Piccadilly. It seems that the bestowing of the name may have started purely informally on a lane which provided an alternative to Oxford Street as a route to the west. It was certainly known as Piccadilly by the middle of the eighteenth century.

The western end of Piccadilly is bounded by Green Park. On the south side, not far from Hyde Park Corner, is a well-known curiosity. This is a porter's rest. It was placed there in 1861 and intended to provide a temporary respite for hard-pressed porters perspiring under the weight of heavy loads. At one time, London possessed a number of such items of street furniture but this is the only one still in existence in the capital and perhaps in the whole of the UK. Perhaps it also came in handy for any passing pallbearers. It bears a plate with the following wording:

At the suggestion of R. A. Slaney, Esq. who for 20 years represented Shrewsbury in Parliament, this Porters Rest was erected in 1861 by the Vestry of St George Hanover Square for the benefit of porters and others carrying burdens. As a relic of a past period in London's history, it is hoped that the people will aid its preservation.

Walk eastwards along Piccadilly and turn right into St James's Street. Building started here in the middle of the seventeenth century. At one time this was the centre of the 'café culture' craze of the late seventeenth and early eighteenth centuries. Coffee houses catered only for men but they were the men-about-town – the literati and glitterati

Porter's Rest, Piccadilly.

– and these establishments became the centre of their social, intellectual, political and business lives. These activities could take place in an atmosphere unsullied by the befuddlement or aggression often associated with the consumption of alcohol. Coffee houses had their vogue but began to go out of fashion as increasingly they started selling alcohol. Some were converted into clubs. St James's Street contains many examples of the new wave of coffee houses which have come on stream in the last ten or fifteen years.

The interest in St James's Street probably lies with its shops. No 'everything for a pound' shops down here. From the earliest days this was a hub of exclusive specialist shops and, remarkably or perhaps not, given the continuing existence of the London rich, two businesses from the eighteenth century are still trading. The first is Berry Brothers and Rudd, wine merchants at No. 3 since 1698. Its arcaded shopfront has a deliberately understated slightly distressed look giving a sense of antiquity and traditional values.

Berry Brothers & Rudd shopfront, St James's Street.

The second surviving shop is Lock & Co., the hatters who have traded at No. 6 since 1765. This firm unleashed the bowler hat on the world. It was designed by an employee, whose surname was Bowler, for a customer who wanted a hat that would not come off when he was following the hunt and jumping fences. The same company had earlier invented the top hat. The first man to wear one in public was arrested and fined £50 for acting in a manner 'calculated to frighten timid people'. Other firms still in business have their roots in the nineteenth century. They include Lobb & Co. at No. 9 who started around 1850 and who have supplied the Crown with boots since 1911. A lamp acts as a shop sign and displays the image of a boot. William Evans, a firm of gunmakers, has been selling their products at No. 67 since 1883. The firm of Robert Lewis has been selling cigars and smokers' requisites at No. 19, Harris have been chemists at No. 29 and at No. 62, Justerini & Brooks have traded wines and spirits, in all cases since the nineteenth century. Nos 37–8 are the address of White's, the oldest of all London clubs. Like many other such establishments, it witnessed innumerable wagers being laid by its wealthy and bored male patrons. They were 'gentlemen' who never did anything as vulgar and tedious as actually working for a living but whose unearned incomes allowed them to stake thousands of pounds on such weighty matters as which one of two drops of rain running down a window would reach the bottom first.

On the west side of St James's Street is St James's Place. At No. 28, a plaque records that William Huskisson (1770–1830) lived on the premises. A politician of some standing, he famously fell out with the Duke of Wellington. Both men were present at the triumphal opening of the Liverpool & Manchester Railway in 1830. Huskisson was keen to effect a reconciliation and he caught sight of the Duke in a railway carriage close by. He climbed down from his own carriage onto an intervening track to make his way across to the Duke and was struck down and injured by the famous locomotive *Rocket*. Although the locomotive rushed him off to receive emergency attention, he died of his injuries. His name lives on, less for his political achievements but on account of being the first person to be killed by a moving railway train.

At the extreme south end of St James's Street on the east side adjacent to Berry Brothers & Rudd an easily missed archway provides access to the small-scale delights of Pickering Place. Its seclusion meant that it was once a favoured place for duels. Note the wall plaque in the entrance explaining that here in the 1840s was located the legation of the Lone Star Republic, as Texas during its brief independence was known.

At the Piccadilly end of St James's Street, Jermyn Street joins from the easterly direction. The building of this street was completed about 1680. On the south side at the junction with Bury Street, the frontage of No. 73 shows a relief of Charles II handing over the deeds to Jermyn, a man who had become immensely rich by assiduously courting all the right people and by skilled wheeling and dealing. The street is renowned for its fashionable specialist shops, especially those catering for the needs of well-heeled men. Among these is No. 97 with a superb Victorian frontage for Harvie & Hudson, bespoke shirtmakers, with colourful tiles and sculpted cartouches above. Other interesting shops include Turnbull & Asser, also shirtmakers at Nos 70–2; Foster & Son, bootmakers at No. 83; Russell & Bromley, retailing footwear at No. 95;

Plaque at the entrance to Pickering Place.

Floris, the perfumers at No. 89 (note the elegant brass nameplate on the stallboard);– Paxton & Whitfield, cheesemongers (at No. 93 since 1835); and Alfred Dunhill, the tobacconists at No. 50. D. R. Harris & Co at No. 29 are believed to run the oldest chemist's business in London. A best-selling line is their 'Pick Me Up'. This is a bottle containing a mixture which will rid the drinker of a hangover. Jermyn Street is worth slow and careful study. Much will be learned about old and attractive shopfronts and also how the other 5 per cent live.

Duke Street crosses Jermyn Street at right angles. Turn north into Duke Street. Where it meets Piccadilly is the world-famous emporium of Fortnum & Mason. On the façade is a clock, put there in 1964, where, as the hour strikes, models of the original eighteenth century partners of the firm emerge from two little boxes and bow to each other. When the chimes have sounded, they bow again and retreat into their boxes.

Trade sign, Jermyn Street.

Turn right along Piccadilly and right again into Eagle Place where on the left there is an interesting piece of *trompe-l'oeil* at street level on a building which appears to be empty and awaiting redevelopment.

Duke of York Street runs south from Jermyn to St James's Square. This was intended to be the centrepiece of a building development financed by Henry Jermyn, Earl of St Albans, on a greenfield site just north of St James's Palace. Work started in the 1660s and the idea was that the residential properties in the area would be for wealthy and prestigious occupants, many of whom would be involved with courtly duties around St James's or in the Palace of Westminster. The scheme was a successful one and for half a century St James's Square was the focal point of the most desirable residential district in London. In the 1680s no fewer than six dukes had residences in the square. Prestige is still attached to the houses round the square but most if not all are now used for

Memorial to WPC Yvonne Fletcher.

commercial purposes. An equestrian statue of William III stands in the gardens in the square (not open to the public at weekends). A foreigner and a dour man little loved by his subjects, especially the Jacobites (those who were loyal to the Stuart pretenders to the throne), William died from injuries sustained when he fell from his horse when it stumbled on a molehill. This fall was greeted with acclaim by the Jacobites who, every year on the anniversary of William's death, used to drink a toast to the mole responsible for the accident. It was described as 'the gentleman in black velvet'.

In the square, opposite No. 5, stands a memorial to WPC Fletcher. In 1984, during a political demonstration, the young policewoman was shot and killed by gunfire coming from this house, then used as the Libyan People's Bureau. This was followed by a siege lasting ten days, but those inside the house claimed diplomatic immunity and were allowed to leave the UK. On the same side of the square is a low stone block. Was it a mounting block?

The north exit from St James's Square is the short Duke of York Street. At No. 2 is the Red Lion, one of London's most notable pubs. This very small pub was built in 1820 and looks pretty unremarkable from the outside. Inside it is a riot of high-quality etched mirrors and accompanying fine mahogany woodwork. Mirrors reflected light and made the place look opulent and seem larger than it actually was. This was intended to attract a 'superior' clientele. The mirrors also allowed the staff to discreetly keep an eye on any prostitutes who might be hawking their wares on the premises. Many magistrates in London in the late nineteenth century were hostile to the licensed trade and would use any excuses to close down 'houses of ill-repute'. One response, therefore, was what is now known as 'transparency'. Publicans were able to demonstrate with such glossy interiors that their premises were properly supervised. It is thought that this pub was extensively refurbished around 1890 and that most of the fittings that can be seen today date from that time.

From St James's Square turn right along Pall Mall. This curious name recalls the ancient game of pall mall, probably French in origin. It involved players hitting a ball along a linear court and through a hanging hoop. A pall mall court formerly stood nearby. This has always been a fashionable street. It has had many famous, or in some cases infamous, residents. When coffee houses were enjoying their vogue, it housed many such establishments. It is now perhaps best known for its clubs, mostly on the south side. They include the Athenaeum, the Reform and the Royal Automobile clubs. A later building stands at No. 79, which was formerly the home of Nell Gwyn, the courtesan who so bewitched Charles II. He whiled away the hours engaged in robust rumpy-pumpy with Nell in a huge bed, whose frame was made of solid silver, placed in the exact centre of a room every inch of the walls of which consisted of mirrors. Pall Mall was the first street in London to be lit by gas, something which had previously been thought ridiculous because it was believed to be impossible.

At the east end of Pall Mall is Waterloo Place. Two mounting blocks can be seen, that on the west side being outside the Athenaeum Club. It bears an inscription which says that it was put there for the convenience of Arthur Wellesley (1769–1852), better known as the Duke of Wellington, at the time when he was still a hero who could do no wrong rather than the querulous and peppery political reactionary he later became.

Duke of Wellington's mounting block, Waterloo Place.

Headstone for Giro, the German shepherd dog lying in a foreign field, Carlton House Terrace.

Just across Carlton House Terrace from Waterloo Place stands the Duke of York's Column, sometimes confused with Nelson's Column, not far away. It was built between 1831 and 1834 and financed by levying a day's pay from all the full-time soldiers in the army, of which the Duke was Commander-in-Chief. It would have been interesting to canvass their views on this involuntary levy. At the time it was said that the Duke was placed at the top of this lofty column in order to put him out of the reach of his creditors (he was notorious for not paying his bills). Close by, just to the right in Carlton House Terrace where the German Embassy once stood, a headstone can be glimpsed. This marks the burial place of the dog belonging to Dr Leopold Von Hoesch. It is dated 1934. The dog's name was Giro and he was, appropriately, a German shepherd. He accompanied his master while the latter was the Ambassador of the Weimar Republic to the Court of St James between 1932 and 1936. Unfortunately for Giro, he died in some corner of a foreign field, but not many dogs get to have a headstone so he shouldn't feel hard done by.

Return to Trafalgar Square and Charing Cross if so wished. As you pass the National Gallery, you might like to know that on the floor near the main entrance is a mosaic of Greta Garbo (1905–1990). She was born Greta Lovisa Gustaffson in Sweden but made her name as glamorous film star in Hollywood in the 1930s.

6

Fleet Street: Lincoln's Inn Fields to St Paul's

This walk starts at Lincoln's Inn Fields and moves south towards Fleet Street then west to Ludgate Hill and St Paul's Cathedral. Fleet Street is one of the most ancient and celebrated thoroughfares in London. Its name was long synonymous with the press, but its history is far richer. For centuries it has been famous for its association with newspapers, printers, stationers, booksellers, taverns, coffee houses, banking houses, the legal profession, places of worship, and exhibitions and processions. Additionally, many famous people have lived in or frequented the street as well as the multitude of alleys, lanes, streets and courts that lead from it. London's second most important river ran close to it and gave the street its name. Carmelite Friars occupied the area between today's Whitefriars Street and the Temple. From the fourteenth century the military order of the Knights Templar was replaced by the legal profession whose members permanently settled in the area.

The Walk

From Holborn tube station walk east along High Holborn and turn into Little Turnstile past the Ship Tavern. It is believed that there was a Ship Tavern near this site since 1549 but the present pub derives its name from the gate or carriage entrance into nearby Lincoln's Inn Fields – once described as 'the haunt of all beggars, rogues, pickpockets, wrestlers, and vile vagrants in London'. A blue plaque outside the pub notes that it became a secret bolt hole for Roman Catholic priests and sympathisers during the religious upheavals of the sixteenth century. However, some priests were discovered hiding in the basement and were condemned to execution – some of them in Lincoln's Inn Fields. Over the years their chilling screams have been heard echoing around the area of Gate Street and the Ship Tavern.

A short walk south along Gate Street will lead into Lincoln's Inn Fields, the largest public square in London. Lincoln's Inn Fields was the site, in 1683, of the public beheading of Lord William Russell, son of the 1st Duke of Bedford, following his implication in the Rye House Plot to assassinate of King Charles II. The executioner was Jack Ketch, who made such a poor job of it that four axe blows were required before the head was separated from the body.

At the southern end of Lincoln's Inn Fields is the Royal College of Surgeons. In the College is the Hunterian Museum which is free to the public (check opening times). The Hunterian Museum – named after John Hunter (1728–1793), one of the most distinguished scientists and surgeons of his day – contains a fascinating mix of comparative anatomy and pathology specimens; complete skeletons, bones, skulls and teeth; dried preparations, corrosion casts and wax teaching models; historical surgical, dental instruments together with modern surgical instruments, and even the skeleton of Jonathan Wild, the hated eighteenth-century criminal whose body was taken from the Tyburn gallows to the anatomy theatre to be publicly dissected as an aggravated punishment.

Victorian drinking
fountain in the
south-east corner of
Lincoln's Inn Fields.

Turn right out of the Royal College of Surgeons and note the Victorian drinking fountain in the south-east corner of Lincoln's Inn Fields. The fountain is in memory of Philip Twells, Barrister at Law of Lincoln's Inn Fields and MP for the City of London.

Take the first right, Serle Street, which meets Carey Street. An old saying, 'being on Carey Street' meant being bankrupt as the bankruptcy court used to be located here. Walk east and turn right into Star Yard. A cast-iron public lavatory (now closed) in the Parisian style is located here.

Head back towards Carey Street, named in memory of one of the street's past residents, the wealthy nobleman Nicholas Carey. Walk directly into Bell Yard and then into Fleet Street. Across the road to the west is No. 1 Fleet Street, now the Royal Bank of Scotland, which occupies the site of two famous buildings: The Devil Tavern and Child's Bank. Child & Co. is the oldest banking house in London dating back to the late seventeenth century. The Devil Tavern was one of the most famous hostelries in London before it was pulled down in 1787.

On the north side of Fleet Street at the corner of Chancery Lane is the statue of 'Kaled' sculptured in white stone. This was placed in the alcove of the pawnbrokers and jewellery emporium of Messrs George Attenborough & Co. in the 1870s when the building was first erected. Kaled is a character from Byron's narrative poem *Lara*:

> The colour of young Kaled went and came,
> The lip of ashes, and the cheek of flame.

On the south side of Fleet Street walk east past Hoare's Bank (No. 37), England's oldest privately owned bank. A number of interesting places along this stretch include the handsome Wren gateway to Middle Temple with the image of a carved sheep above the door dating from 1684. The timber-framed Prince Henry Rooms are at No. 17. This building is one of the few timbered houses in London to survive the Great Fire in 1666 and German bombers in the Second World War. It is named after Prince Henry (elder son of King James I) who would have become King Henry IX had he not died of typhoid at the age of eighteen in 1612. Close to the Prince Henry Rooms is Goslings Bank, which was established in 1650 at the 'Sign of Ye Three Squirrels', a hanging signboard depicting three squirrels which still hangs there. Ye Olde Cock Tavern, which originally stood opposite the present pub, has the old gilt cock over the portal which is believed to have been carved by Grinling Gibbons (1648–1721).

Cross the road onto the north side. Set back from Fleet Street is an alley by the side of the church of St Dunstan-in-the-West called Clifford's Inn Passage. This is all that remains of the last Inn of Chancery. St Dunstan's itself is noted for its clock, which dates from 1671. It has two giant figures said to represent Gog and Magog (according to tradition, the two giants are guardians of the City of London) who strike the hours and quarters with their clubs and turn their heads. The clock was the first public clock in London to have a minute hand and is mentioned in Thomas Hughes's *Tom Brown's Schooldays*, Oliver Goldsmith's *Vicar of Wakefield*, and Charles Dickens's *Barnaby Rudge*.

Disused Parisian-style public lavatory in Star Yard.

Plaque marking the site of the famous Devil Tavern on Fleet Street.

The sign of the 'Three Squirrels' marks
Goslings Bank, founded in 1650.

The famous clock of St Dunstan-in-the-West church with its giant figures, Gog and Magog.

Before leaving St Dunstan's, look out for the drinking fountain (erected in 1860) outside the church and the statue of Queen Elizabeth I. The statue, which was made by William Kirwan around 1586, now stands in the wall at St Dunstan's above the vestry porch. It is the only fragment of old Ludgate that survived the Great Fire.

One of St Dunstan's infamous neighbours was the 'Demon Barber of Fleet Street', Sweeney Todd. Todd is a fictional character who first appeared in a penny dreadful serial entitled *The String of Pearls* (1846–1847). Based partly on urban myth and very tenuous historical fact, Sweeney Todd reputedly had his shop next to the church where the Dundee Courier building now stands. It was in his barber's shop where he murdered his customers by slitting their throats. They were then chopped up and made into meat pies and sold in Mrs Lovett's pie shop in nearby Bell Yard.

Statue of Queen Elizabeth, dating from 1586, outside St Dunstan's church, Fleet Street.

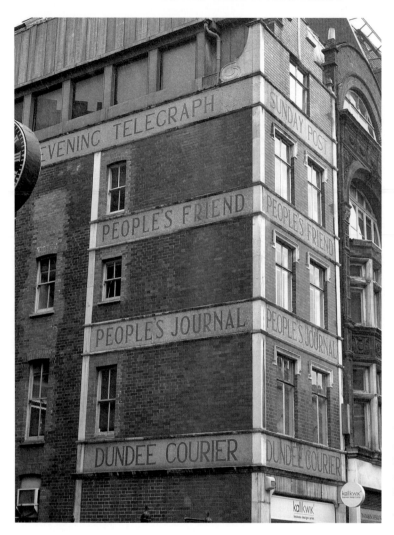

The Dundee Courier building next to St Dunstan's church. This is the site of the fictitious Sweeney Todd's barber's shop.

Moving east we come to Red Lion Court. The court – named after the Red Lion Tavern, which was destroyed in the Great Fire – was once a place of publishing and is where the *Gentleman's Magazine* was published from 1781. The court now consists mostly of offices but there is a K2 telephone box. The first standard public telephone kiosk was produced in concrete in 1920 and was designated K1 (Kiosk No. 1). This design was not of the same family as the familiar red telephone boxes and very few examples remain. The Royal Fine Art Commission was instrumental in the choice of the British standard kiosk because it organised a competition and invited people to submit designs. They selected the design that had been submitted by Giles Gilbert Scott. The Post Office chose to make Scott's winning design in cast iron and to paint it red. It was brought into service as Kiosk No. 2 or K2. From 1926 the K2 was deployed in and around London and the K1 continued to be erected elsewhere. Above the K2 telephone box in Red Lion Court, on the wall of a house, is a printer's sign which

Red Lion Court. A K2
telephone box stands in the
foreground while a printer's
sign can be seen on the
wall in the background; it
depicts a Greek lamp and
dates from the 1820s.

belonged to Abraham Valpy (1787–1854). The sign, dating from the 1820s, depicts a
hand pouring oil into a Greek lamp. It has a motto which reads: *Alere Flammam* (feed
the flame).

Next to Red Lion Court is Johnson's Court which leads into Gough Square where Dr
Johnson lived. His house, now the Johnson Museum, is open to the public. Facing the
house there is a statue of his cat, Hodge, which was erected in 1997. The cat is seated
on Johnson's *Dictionary of the English Language* and has oyster shells at his paws,
a luxury in which Johnson indulged him. Adjoining Gough Square is Gunpowder
Square, complete with a cannon placed there in 1989.

Head back to Fleet Street and cross onto the south side. Walk along Bouverie Street
then turn left into Magpie Alley where there is a significant reminder of medieval Fleet
Street. This is the old Whitefriars church crypt that was discovered during building
works in 1895. It was cleared and restored in the 1920s when this area was redeveloped

The statue of Hodge, Dr Johnson's cat, in Gough Square.

Next to Gough Square is the cannon which has sat in Gunpowder Square since 1989.

Whitefriars church crypt, discovered during building works in 1895.

on behalf of the newspaper *News of the World*. It is possible to view the crypt from outside the building, although there is no direct public access to it.

Walk back onto Fleet Street and head east. The Tipperary pub, which is a few yards along, was built on the site of a monastery and has the River Fleet running beneath it. After the First World War, Irish print workers returning from the trenches renamed it after the popular song 'It's a Long Way to Tipperary' (1912). The Irish origin of the pub goes back to around 1700 when S. G. Mooney & Son's brewery of Dublin bought the pub. It now proclaims itself as 'London's Original Irish Pub' and also boasts that it was the first pub in the whole world outside Ireland to serve Guinness.

At the corner of Fleet Street and Whitefriars Street lived the famous clockmaker Thomas Tompion (1639–1713), known as the father of English watchmaking. When the Royal Observatory was established in 1676, King Charles II selected Tompion to create two clocks, based on an escapement designed by Richard Towneley, that would be wound only once a year. Tompion also made some of the first watches with balance springs. In 1711, he joined in partnership with his apprentice George Graham (1674–1751) who also lived at the same address. A plaque in Fleet Street commemorates both of them.

'London's Original Irish Pub', the Tipperary on Fleet Street.

Mary Queen of Scots House, Fleet Street, built in 1905.

Across the road is the Cheshire Cheese, one of London's best-known and well-loved hostelries. It predates the Great Fire of London, in which it was destroyed, but it was rebuilt in 1667. Next door to the Cheese is Mary Queen of Scots House, built in 1905, where a statue of Mary can be seen overlooking the shop below. The connection with the queen stems from a romantic idea of the developer Sir John Tollemache MP, who was a great admirer of Mary. Next door to the Mary Queen of Scots building stood the old King and Keys public house. Evidence of it can still be seen in its green exterior and the name between the windows.

Continue to walk east past the old *Daily Telegraph* building (built between 1928 and 1931) on the north side; it is now owned by Goldman Sachs Bank. The name of Peterborough Court, which is displayed on the *Telegraph* building, derives from the Abbot of Peterborough who had his lodgings here. Next door is the old *Daily Express* art deco building (1933). On the opposite side of the road is St Bride's church. Stop and

The 'wedding cake' spire of St Bride's church, Fleet Street.

Part of the splendid crypt of St Bride's.

note the steeple. Christopher Wren's 226-foot-high steeple was designed to withstand both lightning and war but it also reputedly inspired the modern wedding cake. When a local baker, William Rich, modelled a wedding cake for his daughter based on the spire, other bakers followed suit and the spire has been known as the 'wedding-cake steeple' ever since. Go inside the church and visit the splendid crypt which displays archaeological remains and two thousand years of history.

Heading east on the south side of Fleet Street is a bust of the journalist and parliamentarian T. P. O'Connor (1848–1929), erected in 1936. O'Connor founded and was the first editor of several newspapers and journals including the *Star* (1887) and *Weekly Sun* (1891). It is believed that he was complicit in knowing about the fake Jack the Ripper letter ('Dear Boss') which was probably written by journalist Frederick Best. Nearby is Salisbury Street where Samuel Pepys was born (look for the plaque).

At the end of Fleet Street is Farringdon Street to the north and New Bridge Street to the south. Under the ground runs the River Fleet which was London's second great river until it became so polluted that it was covered over in stages from the eighteenth century. Jonathan Swift gave a vivid picture of how the Fleet was just a depository for all types of filth:

> Seepings from butcher's stalls, dung, guts and blood,
> Drown'd puppies, stinking sprats, all drenched in mud,
> Dead cats and turnip-tops, come tumbling down into the flood.

It now serves as an underground storm relief sewer continuing its course from Hampstead where it initially flows in two paths before joining up and passing under Belsize Park, Kentish Town and King's Cross and then continuing onto Clerkenwell, Farringdon Street, under Holborn Viaduct, Ludgate Circus and joining the Thames near Blackfriars Bridge. After its journey of over four miles, the Fleet finally flows (more often trickles) into the Thames at Blackfriars through an underground system of brickwork tunnels ranging mostly from eight to twenty feet high.

The historic Temple Bar, near
St. Paul's Cathedral.

Temple Bar as it would have looked on Fleet Street, from a drawing by J. A. Archer.

Before we leave Fleet Street, we might note that it was claimed to have had the first modern public lavatory erected at No. 95 in 1852. It was for men only and was discreetly called a 'public waiting room'. Another, possibly contentious claim is that the first pillar-box was erected in 1855 at the corner of Farringdon Street and Fleet Street. Before this date, people had taken their letters to receiving offices, or relied on itinerant collectors.

From Ludgate Circus walk up Ludgate Hill, one of the three ancient hills of London, the others being Tower Hill and Cornhill. At the top of Ludgate Hill is St Paul's Cathedral. Next to the Cathedral on Paternoster Square the original Temple Bar can be seen. In order to regulate and protect its trade, physical barriers were erected on the main roads into the City. The most famous of these was Temple Bar at the west end of Fleet Street, so named after the Temple church. A bar is first mentioned here in 1293. In 1666 the Great Fire had stopped before it reached Temple Bar but by this time it was in a state of disrepair. In 1672 the new Portland stone structure was completed. Among the less decorative ornamentations that were often placed on Temple Bar were the heads and limbs of those executed for high treason. As the local population and the traffic grew during the nineteenth century, Temple Bar became an obstruction and was removed in 1878. It was bought by the brewer Sir Henry Meux as a gateway to his park and mansion at Theobalds Park, Cheshunt, Hertfordshire. In 2004, after many years of campaigning by the Temple Bar Trust, Temple Bar came home. It now stands adjacent to the north-west tower of St Paul's Cathedral and forms a pedestrian gateway into the redeveloped Paternoster Square.

7

Barbican to Old Bailey

Although one of the shortest of our walks this is nonetheless full of historical interest. For those who like their 'horrible histories', the walk includes tales of executions, hauntings, plague and debauchery. It covers part of Roman London and finishes at the site of Newgate, the most infamous prison in London. At the centre of the walk is Smithfield, which has been the location for tournaments, duels, executions, a plague pit, the famous Bartholomew Fair, and of course the meat market.

The Walk

From Barbican tube station turn right onto Aldersgate Street and head towards the Museum of London. Aldersgate Street is where James I and VI (reigned 1603–1625) entered London as king in 1603 to become the first monarch of both England and Scotland.

The Museum of London (free admission) is worth a visit. The galleries contain hundreds of exhibits from Roman London. In AD 200 Londinium (the Roman City of London) was surrounded by a huge wall with a fort in the north-west corner. The remains of its west gate can be seen beneath the streets next to the Museum of London.

Continue to walk straight on around the large roundabout onto St Martin's Le Grand. The novelist Anthony Trollope designed the famous red pillar box when he worked at the General Post Office on this street. A few yards along on the right-hand side, just past the street called Little Britain, is Postman's Park, a quiet but unique space in the City of London. The park was opened in 1880 on the site of the former churchyard and burial ground of St Botolph's Aldersgate. It was expanded over the next twenty years to incorporate the adjacent burial grounds of Christ Church Greyfriars and St Leonard as well as the site of housing demolished during the widening of Little

Britain. The park's name reflects its popularity among workers from the nearby GPO headquarters.

In one corner of the park, under a canopy, are over fifty plaques with beautiful lettering hand-painted onto Royal Doulton tiles. Each plaque details the untimely death of a heroic but unsung person who died trying to save another life. Those mentioned include Sarah Smith, pantomime artiste who 'died of terrible injuries received when attempting in her inflammable dress to extinguish the flames which had enveloped her companion'; twelve-year-old David Selves of Woolwich who 'supported his drowning playfellow and sank with him clasped in his arms'; William Donald of Bayswater who 'drowned in the Lea trying to save a lad from a dangerous entanglement of weed'; and Alice Ayres 'daughter of a bricklayer's labourer who by intrepid conduct saved 3 children from a burning house in Union Street, Borough at the cost of her own young life'.

The Memorial to Heroic Self Sacrifice was created by the Victorian artist George Frederic Watts (1817–1904). In 1900, the park became the location for this memorial to ordinary people who died saving the lives of others and who might otherwise be forgotten. Following Watts's death in 1904, his wife Mary Watts took over the

Some of the plaques to ordinary heroes in Postman's Park.

Victorian artist G. F. Watts created the Memorial to
Heroic Self Sacrifice in Postman's Park.

Looking towards Smithfield market from St Bartholomew's church.

management of the project and oversaw the building of a small monument to Watts himself.

Leave the park by the entrance behind the memorial, proceed into Little Britain and turn right. Little Britain was built on land owned by the dukes of Brittany and became a location for printers. Follow Little Britain until you enter the open area of West Smithfield.

In the twelfth century William FitzStephen, clerk to Thomas Becket, described West Smithfield as a 'smooth field' where every Friday there is a 'celebrated rendezvous of fine horses to be sold'. Smithfield established a reputation as a livestock market. In addition to the market, Smithfield has a number of other great institutions, notably St Bartholomew's church, St Bartholomew's Hospital – both of which were established in Smithfield by the late twelfth century – and the Charterhouse, which was set up as a Carthusian monastery in 1371. The famous Bartholomew Fair was held in mid to late August, around the time of St Bartholomew's Day (24 August) from 1133 through to 1855. William Wordsworth described the place so vividly in his *Prelude* of 1799:

> I saw ... giants and dwarfs,
> Clowns, conjurors, posture masters, harlequins,
> Amid the uproar of the rabblement,
> Perform their feats ...
> [W]hat anarchy and din
> Barbarian and infernal, 'tis a dream ...
> Monstrous in colour, motion, shape, sight, sound! ...
> Equestrians, tumblers, women, girls, and boys ...
> All moveables of wonder, from all parts,
> Are here—Albinos, painted Indians, Dwarfs,
> The Horse of knowledge, and the learned Pig,
> The Stone-eater, the man that swallows fire,
> Giants, Ventriloquists, the Invisible Girl,
> The Bust that speaks and moves its goggling eyes,
> The Wax-work, Clock-work, all the marvellous craft
> Of modern Merlins, Wild Beasts, Puppet-shows,
> All out-o'-the-way, far-fetched, perverted things,
> All freaks of nature, all Promethean thoughts
> Of man, his dulness, madness, and their feats
> All jumbled up together, to compose
> A Parliament of Monsters, Tents and Booths ...

At the junction of Little Britain and Smithfield is the gateway to the church of St Bartholomew the Great, the oldest parish church in London, founded in 1123. The sixteenth-century timbered house above the gateway was a victim of a First World War zeppelin raid in 1916, then a fire in 1917 in the adjoining warehouse of Evans & Sons, Lescher & Webb, which caused tiles covering the façade to dislodge. The unexpected timber-framed building underneath was then revealed. St Bartholomew's church also has the following associations:

- William Hogarth was baptised here in 1697.
- The church was founded by Rahere, jester to Henry I.
- In 1381 Wat Tyler, leader of the Peasants' Revolt, took refuge here after being stabbed, but he was dragged out and beheaded.
- The church was originally 300 feet longer but Henry VIII demolished the priory in 1539. After the Reformation the church was used as a blacksmith's forge, stable, school, hop-store and printworks.
- It survived the Great Fire of 1666 and the bombs dropped in Zeppelin raids in the First World War and the Blitz in the Second World War.
- It was used as a location in the films *Four Weddings and a Funeral, Shakespeare in Love, The End of the Affair, Amazing Grace, Elizabeth: The Golden Age, The Other Boleyn Girl, Robin Hood: Prince of Thieves* and *Jude.*

The entrance to St Bartholomew the Great church.

Plaque to the Protestant Martyrs executed during the reign of Queen Mary I.

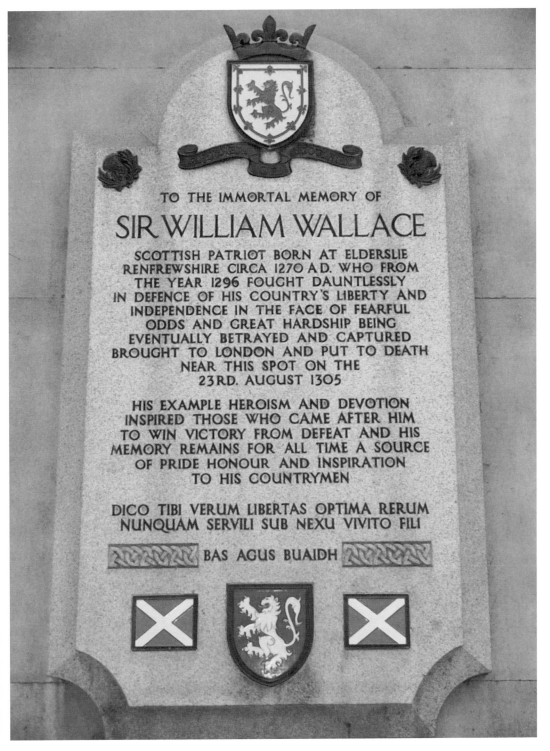

TO THE IMMORTAL MEMORY OF

SIR WILLIAM WALLACE

SCOTTISH PATRIOT BORN AT ELDERSLIE
RENFREWSHIRE CIRCA 1270 AD. WHO FROM
THE YEAR 1296 FOUGHT DAUNTLESSLY
IN DEFENCE OF HIS COUNTRY'S LIBERTY AND
INDEPENDENCE IN THE FACE OF FEARFUL
ODDS AND GREAT HARDSHIP BEING
EVENTUALLY BETRAYED AND CAPTURED
BROUGHT TO LONDON AND PUT TO DEATH
NEAR THIS SPOT ON THE
23RD. AUGUST 1305

HIS EXAMPLE HEROISM AND DEVOTION
INSPIRED THOSE WHO CAME AFTER HIM
TO WIN VICTORY FROM DEFEAT AND HIS
MEMORY REMAINS FOR ALL TIME A SOURCE
OF PRIDE HONOUR AND INSPIRATION
TO HIS COUNTRYMEN

DICO TIBI VERUM LIBERTAS OPTIMA RERUM
NUNQUAM SERVILI SUB NEXU VIVITO FILI

BAS AGUS BUAIDH

Memorial to William Wallace, who was executed at Smithfield in 1305.

The area of West Smithfield is now occupied by a roundabout but it was once an open space for sports, tournaments, markets, fairs and executions. During the reign of Queen Mary I (1553–1558), 270 Protestants were burned here. There is a plaque to the left of St Bartholomew's gateway dedicated to the Protestant Martyrs.

A few yards further along on the wall of St Bartholomew's Hospital is a memorial to the Scottish patriot William Wallace (1272–1305), 'Braveheart', who was executed near to this site. As a punishment for his 'great wickedness', Wallace's heart, liver, lungs and all internal organs were thrown into a fire and burned. Finally, he was decapitated and his carcass was then cut up. His head was set on a pole on London Bridge.

Across the road towards the roundabout a drinking fountain can be seen. This was erected in 1881 in memory of Philip Twells, Member of Parliament for the City of London. The Metropolitan Drinking Fountain Association became the Metropolitan Drinking Fountain and Cattle Trough Association in 1867 when it started providing cattle troughs. Smithfield's long history as a livestock market is partly reflected here as cattle were still arriving on foot to the meat market and were often in a very sorry state when they did.

From the William Wallace memorial walk a few yards west. On the left is the King Henry VIII entrance to St Bartholomew's Hospital. This is the only statue of Henry VIII on public display in London. It was erected in this new gatehouse in 1702 to acknowledge that in 1546 Henry had granted St Bartholomew's to the City of

The Metropolitan Drinking Fountain and Cattle Trough Association provided this cattle trough in West Smithfield.

The only public statue of Henry VIII in London stands above the entrance to St Bartholomew's Hospital, Smithfield.

The Watch House on Giltspur Street was built to deter grave robbers.

London. The two figures on the broken pediment represent lameness and sickness. St Bartholomew's is the oldest surviving hospital in England, existing on the same site for almost 900 years. It survived both the Great Fire of London and the Blitz. The only medieval part remaining is the tower of the church of St Bartholomew the Less.

Continue walking, then turn left into Giltspur Street. Look out for the Watch House. This watch house was built overlooking the churchyard of St Sepulchre's in the seventeenth century to stop grave robbers. This area was particularly active for Resurrection Men (body snatchers) who met in nearby pubs, notably the Fortune of War (demolished in 1910) on nearby Cock Lane, to discuss the sale of bodies with surgeons.

On the west side of Giltspur Street is Cock Lane. At the junction of this street is the Golden Boy of Pye Corner, a life-size gold statue of a small boy. During the seventeenth century, this location was considered one of London's most disreputable sites. Indeed, Cock Lane (originally known as Cokkes Lane) was home to a number of legal brothels. The Golden Boy was erected at the limit of the Great Fire. Unlike Sir Christopher Wren's Monument, which blames (or did until the text was removed in 1831) the fire upon the malice of Papists, the Golden Boy blames the fire on the sin of gluttony. Based on this unusual notion, that greed and intemperance brought about the fire as a punishment from God, the Golden Boy was erected with the following inscription: 'This Boy is in Memmory Put up for the late FIRE of LONDON Occasion'd by the Sin of Gluttony'. The Golden Boy was originally affixed to the front of the Fortune of War pub.

Cock Lane was once notorious for prostitution, and although now a relatively uninteresting thoroughfare, it was the location of a famous haunting that centred on a young child called Elizabeth Parsons. Number 33 Cock Lane was once the home of William Parsons but the house has long been demolished. In October 1762 crowds gathered nightly in the narrow lane to witness a possible spectral event, no matter what the weather was like. The poltergeist was said to be the spirit of a former resident, Fanny Kent, who had been murdered by her husband. The tenant of the house at the time of the disturbance was William Parsons who had invented the ghost story for the purpose of blackmailing the deceased's woman's husband. The disturbance was finally traced to Parson's eleven-year-old daughter, Elizabeth, and Parsons himself was prosecuted and pilloried.

Continue along Giltspur Street up to the junction with Newgate Street. On the corner is the Viaduct Tavern which is opposite the Central Criminal Court (Old Bailey). The Old Bailey stands on the site of what was part of the infamous Newgate Prison. The Viaduct Tavern was named after the nearby Holborn viaduct, which was opened by Queen Victoria in 1869. Built in the same year, the Viaduct is a Victorian pub and this is reflected in its furnishings – engraved glass, gilded mirrors, glazed partitions, several enormous Roman columns proudly holding up the ceiling, and walls made of marble. Across the road is the church of St Sepulchre-without-Newgate referred to in the nursery rhyme 'Oranges and Lemons': 'when will you pay me say the bells of Old Bailey'. Beneath the Viaduct Tavern are what appear to be prison cells. Some claim that these were the remains of the old Newgate Prison, but this is unlikely. Other accounts

The Golden Boy of Pye Corner stands at the junction of Cock Lane and Giltspur Street.

The Viaduct Tavern stands opposite the site of Newgate Prison.

London's first public drinking
fountain, set into the railings of
St Sepulchre-without-Newgate.

Execution Bell in St Sepulchre's.

say they may be part of the old Compter prison. The less exciting view is that they are just a combination of old coal cellars and wine vaults. Well, at least they are reputed to be haunted.

Across the road from the Viaduct is London's first public drinking fountain, which dates from 1859 when Samuel Gurney MP set up aforementioned Metropolitan Drinking Fountain Association to provide free water and thus discourage the drinking of alcohol. Like many, it was sited opposite a pub. Set into the railings of St Sepulchre's church, it asks the user to replace the cup, which, unusually, retains its chain.

St Sepulchre's church, the largest of London's parish churches, has its origins in the twelfth century. It was rebuilt in the fifteenth century, destroyed in 1666 in the Great Fire and rebuilt again by Sir Christopher Wren. Only small parts of its medieval stonework remained after the fire. In 1612 Robert Dow, a tailor, left an annual endowment to the church to ensure that the bellman of the church never failed to sound the bell on the eve of execution days and to ring it again as the cart carrying the condemned left Newgate for Tyburn the following morning. At midnight before the executions, the sexton walked solemnly through the passageway and stood outside the cells of the condemned. There he rang the bell twelve times and recited a warning prayer. Today, the bell is encased in glass and on display inside the church. John Smith, the Englishman who was protected by Pocahontas in the New World, worshipped at St Sepuchre's and is buried there.

There is a City of London plaque opposite the Viaduct Tavern that rather misleadingly states, 'Site of Newgate. Demolished 1777'. In fact this refers to the final pulling down of the last of the jumble of ancient buildings, most of which had either evolved over a long time or been adapted for prison use. Reconstruction had actually started in 1770

A nineteenth-century execution outside Newgate Prison.

and Newgate had hardly been completed when, during the Gordon Riots of 1780, large parts of it were torn down by ravening, drunken mobs. Very quickly it was completely rebuilt in a grand style by the architect George Dance the Younger. Despite its grand exterior, the conditions experienced by the prisoners and the general corruption of the regime under which it was run soon meant that, if anything, the reborn Newgate had an even more fearsome reputation than its predecessor. Its notoriety led to a parliamentary enquiry in 1814 and it was one of the first prisons to which the reformer Elizabeth Fry turned her attention. Improvements were slow in coming. Its overcrowding was somewhat relieved by the opening of Holloway Prison in 1852. In Newgate's last years it was used mainly for prisoners committed to trial at the Old Bailey and for those awaiting execution. The last public execution outside Newgate took place on 26 May 1868 when a young Fenian, Michael Barrett, was hanged by the famous executioner William Calcraft. It closed as a prison in 1881. Although the prison is long gone, there is still a tiny passage behind the wall at the end of Amen Court that was named 'Dead Man's Walk'. This is where prisoners were led to their executions. Some ninety-seven condemned men are buried beneath the stone flags of the corridor that connected the prison with the adjoining courts next door.

8

Newgate to Tyburn:
Old Bailey to Marble Arch

The historic route between Newgate and Tyburn was the journey that many condemned felons took on their way to the infamous 'Tyburn Tree' gallows until 1783. Thousands of spectators often lined the route to express their contempt and disapproval of the condemned. However, the crowd were also, on occasion, capable of showing sympathy to those they considered to be heroes or merely unfortunate. This walk is approximately three miles long and includes busy areas. A good time to do it would be early on a Sunday morning. The walk starts outside the Central Criminal Court, commonly known as the Old Bailey.

The Central Criminal Court was opened in 1834 and the complex of buildings of which it is composed has been added to since that time. After many delays, the new building, designed in the neo-Baroque style by E. W. Mountford, was finally opened by King Edward VII in 1907. It has witnessed innumerable famous trials, among the most celebrated of which were those of Oscar Wilde (1895), Hawley Harvey Crippen (1910), George Joseph Smith, the 'Brides in the Bath' murderer (1915), William 'Lord Haw-Haw' Joyce (1945), John Reginald Christie (1953) and the 'Yorkshire Ripper' Peter Sutcliffe (1981). The Old Bailey was severely damaged by German bombs in 1941 and witnessed a number of IRA bomb attacks in 1973. One curious tradition still observed on certain occasions at the Old Bailey is that of the judges carrying posies of sweet-smelling flowers. This recalls the use of nosegays in earlier days as a way of warding off the foul smells and what were thought of as lethal miasmas that Newgate prisoners brought with them when they came into court. Atop the Old Bailey is a massive bronze statue portraying Justice. The proceedings of the Old Bailey from 1674 to 1913 can be found on the excellent Old Bailey Online website.

The Walk

Proceed along High Holborn to Holborn Viaduct, once wryly but wrongly described as 'the world's first flyover'. This was completed in 1869 at a cost of about £2.5 million. The viaduct crosses Farringdon Street and epitomises Victorian civic pride with its allegorical bronze statues. On the north side the statues represent 'Commerce' and 'Agriculture' while those on the south depict 'Science' and 'Fine Arts'. Curiously there were four rather Italianate yet semi-Gothic houses erected at the four corners of the viaduct. These were decorated with statues, and those that can be viewed today depict Henry FitzAilwyn (died 1212) who was the first mayor of the City and Sir Thomas Gresham (1519–1579) who is immortalised as the founder of the Royal Exchange and Gresham College. The others are of Sir William Walworth – the perfidious Lord Mayor of London who stabbed Wat Tyler – and Sir Hugh Myddleton, who was responsible for the New River which brought the City an excellent water supply from Hertfordshire in the early seventeenth century.

On the south side we pass the City Temple. This is the only Nonconformist church in the City and its origins can be traced back to 1640. However, the present building dates only from 1874, replacing an earlier chapel located in Poultry. After considerable bomb damage in the Second World War, the City Temple was rebuilt and enlarged in 1955–8. Close by is the church of St Andrew's, Holborn. Various restorations were made but the church was largely obliterated in the Blitz. In fact, only the tower and walls were left standing. Rebuilding and restoration were completed in 1961. On the west front of St Andrew's can be seen statues of schoolchildren from the parish school which was in nearby Hatton Garden.

We are now at Holborn Circus. Causing something of an obstacle to the free flow of traffic at this busy intersection is an equestrian statue of Prince Albert in bronze, erected in 1874. This has wittily been described as 'the most polite statue in London' because, rather curiously, it is doffing its hat towards the City of London.

Hatton Garden can be seen to the north. It has gained international fame as the headquarters of London diamond traders and takes its name from Sir Christopher Hatton (c. 1540–1591) who was a statesman and survivor in the shifting sands of Elizabethan politics. At No. 57 Hatton Garden, Hiram Maxim invented his machine gun in the early 1880s. Further up, on the corner of Cross Street is the façade of an old charitable bluecoat school, designed by Wren in 1696, with statues of pupils on the frontage. Blue was used for the uniforms of charity-school children because it was the cheapest dye available for clothing.

Return and continue to walk along Holborn. On the north side the headquarters of the Prudential Assurance Company comes into view. This was built on part of the site of Furnival's Inn, one of the Inns of Chancery, and was originally designed by Alfred Waterhouse in something of a Gothic revival style. The original building came into use in 1879 but what can be seen today is a reconstruction which has been added to ever since. Charles Dickens lived at Furnival's Inn between 1834 and 1837 and there is a plaque to that effect in the courtyard of the Prudential building. He began writing *The Pickwick Papers* while he resided here.

Figures of bluecoat children in Hatton Gardens.

Brooke Street is the last road on the north of Holborn before Gray's Inn Road. This takes its name from Fulke Greville, who became Lord Brooke in 1620 and built a mansion here (now long-demolished) which he modestly named after himself. A short distance up Brooke Street is a blue plaque on No. 39 indicating that the poet Thomas Chatterton (1752–1770) died there – he committed suicide with arsenic. At No. 20 Brooke Street, William Friese-Greene (1855–1921) had a photographic laboratory where, in 1889, he gave the first ever demonstration of moving pictures.

At the junction of Holborn with Gray's Inn Road the picturesque Staple Inn comes into view on the south side. Although this has been rebuilt on a number of occasions, it provides a very good idea of how many of the half-timbered structures of Tudor London would have looked. It was one of the Inns of Chancery and not a hostelry. In 1886 the government bought part of Staple Inn to provide an extension to the Patent Office. Another part was sold to the Prudential Assurance Company. There is a quaint notice in the entrance gateway forbidding horses to enter or children to play in the precincts. This notice reads: 'The Porter has orders to prevent all clothes, men and others from calling articles for sale, also rude children playing, etc. No horses allowed within this inn.' At the time of writing (April 2010) this notice, for whatever reason, has been removed.

Gray's Inn Road is the eastern boundary of Gray's Inn, one of the four great Inns of Court originally established to provide teaching and accommodation for students of the law.

At No. 22 High Holborn stands the Cittie of York pub. There has been a drinking house on this site since 1430, but what can be seen today is the result of a further rebuilding in the 1890s. The bar is one of the longest in Britain and on a high gallery can be seen a number of enormous vats which Henekey's, the wine merchants and former owners, used for housing their wines and spirits. There is a high arched ceiling of almost cathedral-like appearance. Other curiosities of this pub are a number of cubicles with swing doors where lawyers could have private meetings with clients over a drink or meal. Perhaps most curious of all is a stove dating from 1815 from which the smoke escapes by means of a vent under the floor.

High Holborn is the continuation of Holborn to Shaftesbury Avenue. On the south side at No. 208 stands the Princess Louise. This pub, named after Queen Victoria's fourth daughter, was built in 1872. Spatially this is a magnificent pub but what marks it out are its interior décor and fittings. There is a riot of etched and decorative glass, superb pictorial tiling, polished woodwork and gold embossed mirrors. The Princess Louise is a splendid example of Victorian pub design and architecture and should on no account be missed by pub aficionados. Also on the south side is a newish pub by the name of Pendrell's Oak. This name recalls the Pendrell family who owned Boscobel House in Shropshire. They were devoted supporters of the Royalist cause in the Civil War and it was to Boscobel that Charles II fled after the Battle of Worcester on 3 September 1651. The pub is close to Pendrell House where the Meteorological Office's London Weather Centre is located.

On the left is the alley known as Little Turnstile. This probably recalls the revolving stiles that were placed at the four corners of Lincoln's Inn Fields to ensure that the cattle which grazed there could not escape. Later these stiles may have helped to ensure that other animals being driven through the area to the meat market at Smithfield did not stray into these hallowed grounds. Little Turnstile gives access to Lincoln's Inn Fields where at Nos 59–60 an LCC plaque commemorates the fact that Spencer Perceval (1762–1812) lived there. He was Prime Minister when he was assassinated by a bankrupt businessman who blamed Perceval for his economic misfortunes.

Lincoln's Inn Fields is worth a short diversion. On the north side of Lincoln's Inn Fields, which were laid out in the early 1640s, is the somewhat undersung Sir John Soane's Museum. Soane was a man of humble origins who accumulated an extraordinarily eclectic hoard of artistic and antiquarian items, including Gothic fantasies, Egyptian sarcophagi, paintings by Canaletto, Watteau and Wiliam Hogarth. On the south side of Lincoln's Inn Fields is the Royal College of Surgeons which on its first floor contains the Hunterian Museum. This exhibits some of the enormous collection of anatomical specimens and bodily parts accumulated by the avid Scottish scientist, surgeon, physiologist and anatomist John Hunter (1728–1793). The most fascinating exhibit is probably the skeleton of the renowned Irish giant Charles Byrne, who was almost 8 feet tall. Placed next to Byrne's mortal remains are those of a midget

Inn sign for the
Victorian pub, the
Princess Louise.

named Caroline Crachami, otherwise known as the 'Sicilian Fairy', who was only 23
inches tall when she died at the age of nine.

Head back onto High Holborn, which at this point is crossed at right angles by
Kingsway and Southampton Row. A feature that is visible as we cross Kingsway
is the northern end of the tram subway that used to run to the Embankment. This
subway, possibly unique in Britain, linked the north and south London tram systems
and allowed trams to avoid road congestion by passing through what was in effect an
underpass. The last tram to use the subway did so on 5 July 1952. As late as 1950, the
subterranean Holborn tram station was lit by powerful gas lamps, the loud hissing of
which helped to add to the very tangible atmosphere of this curious facility.

Close by to the west on the north side of High Holborn once stood British Museum
Underground station on what was originally the Central London Railway. It was
opened in 1900 but in 1933 the new Holborn station came into use and the British

Museum stop closed. Before it did, however, stories circulated that the station was haunted by a spectre in the form of an Egyptian mummy that had escaped from the museum itself. Rather irresponsibly, a national newspaper offered cash for anyone prepared to stay on the station overnight. The now grubby white tiled walls can just be discerned from Central Line trains as they run between Holborn (Kingsway) and Tottenham Court Road stations.

Shaftesbury Avenue dates from the mid-1880s and is named after Anthony Ashley Cooper (1801–1885), 7th Earl of Shaftesbury. At the junction of High Holborn and Shaftesbury Avenue, Endell Street can be seen on the left and this contains the Swiss Protestant church founded in 1762 where Sunday services are conducted in French. Beyond Endell Street is Bow Street, where a courthouse was opened in 1748 and where Henry Fielding and his half-brother, the blind Sir John Fielding were magistrates. It was here that the Bow Street Runners started their operations. The Bow Street Magistrates Court stood on the site, but its building is no longer used to administer the law.

We proceed along the old route up St Giles High Street. On the south side is the Angel pub. This is an ancient hostelry although it was rebuilt in 1898 and was previously known as The Bowl. It is said to have been one of the major stopping places for condemned felons and their hangers-on making their way from Newgate to Tyburn. Immediately on the left is the church of St Giles in the Fields topped by a fine steeple 150 feet high. This has its origins in the chapel of a leper colony established in 1101. St Giles is not far from where the Great Plague of London started in 1665 and in just one month in that year, 1,391 burials were recorded in its churchyard. On the west front of St Giles the name of its architect, Henry Flitcroft, is displayed prominently on a frieze while close by is what can best be described as a stone lychgate, erected in 1804. This rather curious structure incorporates a wooden bas-relief of the Resurrection which was carved in 1687 and may be based on Michelangelo's *Last Judgment* in the Sistine Chapel of Rome. The interior contains many fine seventeenth- and eighteenth-century furnishings.

From St Giles High Street our route passes Andrew Borde Street where St Giles' Hospital stood before it was dissolved. Very briefly we join New Oxford Street. This had been completed in 1847 and involved the knocking down of some of London's most festering slums. Now we enter Oxford Street, which has always been a traditional route out of London to the west.

Oxford Street divides Marylebone and Fitzrovia on the north with Mayfair and Soho to the south. To the thousands of people who walk, shop or commute along the 1.5-mile stretch of Oxford Street today there is little evidence of its pre-Victorian history. Oxford Street's reputation as one of the world's most famous, busiest and longest shopping streets has its origins in the late eighteenth century. It was also in the earlier eighteenth century that this old Roman road acquired the name Oxford Street. Until the 1750s it was variously called the Uxbridge, Oxford, Worcester, or Tyburn Road. The road, which was administered by a turnpike trust from 1721, was described as 'a deep hollow road, full of sloughs; with here and there a ragged house, the living place of cut-throats'. From 1718 piecemeal development along Oxford Street started at the Tottenham Court Road end. In the twenty years after 1763 the expansion

St Giles in the Field church – a stopping place for condemned criminals on their way to Tyburn.

astonished foreign visitors. The street was entering an age of refinement defined by the fashionable houses to the north and south-western end as well as the shops, coffee houses, public houses, 'lacquered coaches ... pavement inlaid with flag-stones' and the 'splendidly-lit shop fronts'.

The first road junction along Oxford Street on the north side is with the short Hanway Street. This is probably named after Jonas Hanway (1712–1786) who was assured immortality when he was the first Englishman to venture out onto the streets of the capital carrying an umbrella to protect him from the rain and incurring huge ridicule in doing so. At No. 22 there is a Westminster City Council plaque on the house where Jessie Matthews, actress and dancer, was born. The last role for which she is remembered is as Mrs Dale in the long-running radio soap opera *Mrs Dale's Diary*, which later became *The Dales*.

About one third of the way along Oxford Street is the junction with Regent Street. This street was part of an ambitious scheme by, among others, John Nash (1752–1835),

The River Tyburn, which can be seen in Grays Antiques on Davies Street.

the town planner and architect, to connect what came to be called Regent's Park with the official residence of the Regent, Carlton House. Today Regent Street remains one of the leading shopping areas of central London. Visible from Oxford Circus along the east side of Regent Street is Liberty's. This world famous, albeit idiosyncratic, emporium can trace its origins to Arthur Lasenby Liberty, who started selling oriental fabrics and other goods in Regent Street in the 1870s.

Just before the intersection of Oxford Street and Regent Street, Argyll Street comes in from the south. Close to Oxford Street are Nos 8 and 10 Argyll Street. These display blue plaques commemorating Washington Irving and William Roy respectively. Washington Irving (1783–1859) was an American who was also something of an Anglophile. He lived for some time in London and knew many of the leading figures in art and literature. He is perhaps best known for his American adaptation of German folk tales such as 'Rip van Winkle' and 'The Legend of Sleepy Hollow'.

Immediately after Argyll Street stands Oxford Circus tube station. This has largely managed to retain the façade with glazed dark ruby red tiling which was so characteristic of the work of Leslie W. Green, appointed in 1903 as the architect of the Underground Electric Railways Company of London.

Moving westwards along Oxford Street, New Bond Street soon joins from the south. Before Bond Street station is Davies Street. A short walk along here is Grays Antiques. When the proprietors of the building moved in, the basement was under six feet of water. The cause of this was a running tributary to the Thames – the famous

William Hogarth's depiction of an execution day at Tyburn in the eighteenth century.

hidden River Tyburn, which now runs underground. A short stretch of the river can be seen.

At the junction of Oxford Street and Edgware Road a lamp-post bears a plaque, erected by Westminster City Council, which is inscribed with the legend, 'Site of Tyburn Gallows. For four centuries [*sic*] Londoners celebrated executions on this spot with public hangings'. Four centuries seems something of an understatement. In the complex of roads and the bedlam of traffic which surrounds Marble Arch, there is a short slip road, used only by buses, called Tyburn Way. Marble Arch is a well-known London landmark, although many people are not aware that there are three small rooms inside the arch that were used as a police station until 1950, first for the royal constables of the park and later the Metropolitan Police.

A blue plaque in the traffic island at the junction of Edgware Road and Bayswater Road marks the site of where the fixed gallows is thought to have stood from 1571 to 1759. The gallows were known as the 'Tyburn Tree' but were replaced by a moveable gallows where a toll house was built on a site for the turnpike road. Few reminders of Tyburn exist except Tyburn Walk near Marble Arch and Tyburn Convent along Bayswater Road. Also, further up Edgware Road at No. 195 is a branch of Lloyds Bank where a stone gatepost is on display in the window. This is from one of the Tyburn toll gates.

9

Bankside: London Bridge to Blackfriars Bridge

Bankside is the area encompassed by Blackfriars Road on the west, Southwark Street to the south and London Bridge to the east. Bankside has a rich and diverse history and has, over the centuries, reinvented itself on many occasions. In the medieval period it was a residential area of ecclesiastical houses and mansions before establishing a reputation for brothels, bear baiting and theatre. This in turn gave way to varied activities including lime-burning, tanning, brewing, wharf work, ferry services, printing, railway engineering, foundries, and countless small industries. Bankside has provided inspiration for literature, hospitals for the poor, and it has one of the finest medieval buildings in London in Southwark Cathedral.

Following industrial decline after the Second World War, Bankside remained largely derelict and neglected. By the millennium it had become one of London's main tourist honeypots. With the establishment of attractions such as the Globe Theatre, Tate Modern, Millennium Bridge, Clink Prison, Bankside Gallery, replica of the *Golden Hind*, varied restaurants, and the adjacent Borough Market, the changes in Bankside have been among the most dynamic in London.

The Walk

Our walk starts at London Bridge tube station from where we head west, across Borough High Street towards Southwark Cathedral. Southwark Cathedral has been a place of Christian worship for over a thousand years. From the Dissolution in 1540 until 1905 it was known as the parish church of St Saviour and in 1905 it became Southwark Cathedral. It is London's second oldest church, after Westminster Abbey, and one of the most important medieval buildings in South London. Southwark Cathedral houses many memorials and tombs. Not surprisingly, given its close proximity to many of the playhouses that were located in Bankside, several prominent actors and writers are commemorated in the church. There are memorials to lesser-known individuals such as Lionel Lockyer (*c.* 1600–1672) a seventeenth-century quack doctor who was famous in his time for his miracle pills that he claimed included sunbeams as ingredients. Part of the epitaph on his tomb reads:

Here Lockyer: lies interr'd enough: his name
Speakes one hath few competitors in fame …
His virtues & his PILLS are soe well known
That envy can't confine them under stone.
But they'll survive his dust and not expire
Till all things else at th'universall fire.
This verse is lost, his PILL Embalmes him safe
To future times without an Epitaph.

The memorial to Lionel Lockyer, seventeenth-century quack doctor, in Southwark Cathedral.

Next to Southwark Cathedral is Borough Market. The present buildings of the market were designed in 1851, with additions made in the 1860s and an entrance designed in the art deco style added on Southwark Street in 1932. A refurbishment began in 2001. The area around Borough Market became the setting for a number of film scenes in *Bridget Jones's Diary* (2001) and *Bridget Jones: The Edge of Reason* (2004). A flat above the Globe pub on Bedale Street near Borough Market was where the eponymous heroine lived her single life. Across from Bedale Street the shops were transformed into the cab office, the newsagent and the Greek restaurant where Daniel Cleaver (Hugh Grant) and Mark Darcy (Colin Firth) fight during a birthday party. Bridget walks despondently through Borough Market after discovering Cleaver with Lara (Lisa Barbuscia), and the Clink Wharf Apartments on Clink Street were used as Cleaver's flat.

West from Borough Market is Stoney Street. To the left is Park Street which runs parallel to Bankside and contains a number of interesting features for the visitor who wishes to walk the length of the street. Look out for the site of the Rose Theatre (a blue plaque at 56 Park Street marks the site). Over 700 small objects, including jewellery, coins, tokens and fragment of the moneyboxes used to collect entrance money from the audience, were also found on the site and are now housed in the Museum of London. A plaque in Park Street marks an 'international incident' that took place in 1850. This concerned General Haynau, well known as the despotic and cruel dictator of Austria, who came to London and went to see the huge Anchor Brewery at Southwark. The workers were incensed to hear that the tyrant was on the premises and they attacked him and gave him a severe beating. With some companions, Haynau fled and was forced to hide in a dustbin in a pub yard while his pursuers searched in vain for 'Hyena', as they disparagingly called him. He was eventually smuggled away from the scene of his humiliation in a police boat.

Also on Park Street is the original site of the Southwark Globe Theatre which was discovered in 1989 beneath the car park at the rear of Anchor Terrace. The site of the theatre is marked by a plaque, while some information boards as well as a useful granite line show the original theatre location. Park Street has been frequently used for scenes in films such as *Keep the Aspidistra Flying* (1997), *Howards End* (1992) and *Lock Stock and Two Smoking Barrels* (1998). In *Lock, Stock...* the gang's hideout is 15 Park Street, and the street also features in *Entrapment* (1999), starring Sean Connery and Cartherine Zeta-Jones, as well as David Cronenberg's *Spider* (2002) in which it is the site of Spider's (Ralph Fiennes) childhood.

For the purpose of this walk we continue along Stoney Street and onto Bankside. In St Mary Overie Dock is a replica of Sir Francis Drake's famous ship the *Golden Hind* (or *Golden Hinde*). The original *Golden Hind* became famous as Drake's flagship during his three-year voyage around the world between 1577 and 1580. The replica is a fully working ship that was launched in Devon in 1973. It has sailed over 140,000 miles and in 1979–80 it retraced Drake's voyage around the world. Between 1984 and 1985 it circumnavigated the British Isles and then sailed to the Caribbean.

Proceed along Clink Street. On the left are the remains of Winchester Palace. This was the London residence of the bishops of Winchester from the twelfth century

Plaque in Park Street commemorating the 'International Incident' in which General Haynau was set upon by Southwark dray-men.

The replica of the *Golden Hind* in St Mary Overie Dock, Pickfords Wharf, Bankside.

The rose window in the
remains of Winchester
Palace.

until the Civil War of the 1640s. Southwark was the largest town in the old diocese
of Winchester (Winchester being the old Saxon capital) and most of the brothels in
Southwark were owned by the Bishop of Winchester.

In 1941 German incendiary bombs fell on the flour warehouse at the south-west
corner of the junction of Clink Street and Stoney Street, completely gutting the
building. The wall of the fourteenth-century Great Hall and the rose window, which
was first restored in 1972, are all that remain above ground today. Winchester Square,
once the courtyard of Winchester House, is now effectively a service area to Palace
House, overlooking the dock. It is a Scheduled Ancient Monument managed by
English Heritage.

As we approach the River Thames, the first building encountered is the Anchor pub,
located at 1–2 Bankside. This is one of the oldest surviving buildings in the area. It
suffered severe fires in 1750 and 1876, being rebuilt on each occasion, but ironically is

One of a number of
old cannon bollards
around Bankside.

perhaps best known as the place from which a horrified Samuel Pepys in 1666 watched
the Great Fire wreaking its destruction through the city he loved on the opposite side
of the river. Even at that distance, the heat of the conflagration could be felt and he
was showered with sparks. Dr Johnson knew The Anchor well. He was very friendly
with the Thrale family who at that time owned the nearby brewery, and they allowed
him a room there in which he could work away at the compiling of his dictionary.

Keep a look out for a number of cannon bollards en route. There are five cast-iron
cannon posts located in the front of 21 and 23 Park Street and inscribed 'Clink 1812'.
Another is located at the west corner of Rose Alley and Park Street and is inscribed
and painted in black and white stripes. A cast-iron cannon bollard is also located at the
west corner of Bear Gardens and Park Street. These are Grade II listed monuments.

To the west is Southwark Bridge. By the eighteenth century, London Bridge simply
could not cope effectively with the amount of traffic needing to cross the river and

there were calls for a new bridge. In 1819 John Rennie's bridge opened for public use. In 1913 work started on a replacement bridge which was officially opened on 6 June 1921. As we pass under the arches at the Bankside end of Southwark Bridge, there are a series of mural pictures depicting the Frost Fairs that used to be held on the frozen river during the numerous bouts of extremely cold weather that were a feature of the past.

Proceeding west along Bankside we have a magnificent view of buildings across the River Thames in the City of London. Look out for a narrow passage on the left-hand side called Bear Garden. On the corner of Bear Garden is a ferryman's seat. The seat was constructed for the convenience of Bankside watermen who operated ferrying services across the river as the city only had London Bridge which crossed over the river. Ferrymen were kept in business by the traffic of people who came to Bankside to visit the brothels (or 'stews'), the bear-baiting and the theatres. The plaque above the seat states that its age is unknown but its origin is thought to be ancient.

Along Bear Gardens in August 2004 the Museum of London Archeology Service (MoLAS) uncovered remains of the actual Bear Gardens arena, owned by James Davies in the seventeenth century, during an excavation. Today a single red-brick house set among warehouses and offices on Bear Gardens, just a few paces from both the Globe and the Rose, marks the site of the last bear-baiting ring on Bankside. The house on Bear Gardens is now the Globe Education Centre. The diarist John Evelyn recorded a visit to Bankside on 16 June 1670:

> I went with some friends to the Bear Garden, where there was cock-fighting, dog-fighting, bear and bull-baiting, it being a famous day for all these butcherly sports, or rather barbarous cruelties. The bulls did exceeding well, but the Irish wolfe-dog exceeded, which was a tall greyhound, a stately creature indeede, who beat a cruel mastiff. One of the bulls toss'd a dog full into a lady's lap, as she sat in one of the boxes at a considerable height from the arena. Two poore dogs were kill'd, and so all ended with the ape on horseback, and I, most heartily weary of the rude and dirty pastime, which I had not seen, I think, in twenty years before.

Continuing west along Bankside we pass the modern reconstruction of Shakespeare's Globe. In 1949 the American-born actor-director-producer Sam Wanamaker came to London looking for the site of the original Globe and was disappointed not to find a more lasting memorial to Shakespeare and his theatre. As a first step in bringing the Bard back to the bank of the Thames, Wanamaker acquired some rights to nearby property and persuaded the Southwark Borough Council to allow him to operate a tent theatre in which he mounted Shakespearean and contemporary dramas. By 1970, from these beginnings, the International Shakespeare Globe Centre project emerged. In 1987 building work began on site, and in 1993 the construction of the new theatre began. After twenty-three years of fundraising, research into the appearance of the original Globe and planning the reconstruction with architect Theo Crosby, Sam Wanamaker died on 18 December 1993, before the theatre finally opened in 1997. Shakespeare's Globe has a capacity for more than 1,500 people, 500 of them standing

Ferryman's seat at the corner of Bankside and Bear Gardens.

in the yard at the actors' feet, many of them close enough to reach out and touch the players.

Slightly west of the Globe a tall white house with a plaque above the door can be seen. This is No. 49 Bankside, variously known as Wren's House or Cardinal's Wharf. Since the publication of Gillian Tindall's book in 2007, it might also be referred to as *The House by the Thames*. The plaque above the door describes the house as the place where Christopher Wren lived but this is not quite true, as Wren never actually lived there. The association with Wren is based on the notion that he stayed at 49 Bankside to chart the progress of St Paul's Cathedral on the other side of the river. However, it was in fact from another house a few yards further west that he watched his great dome develop. This residence was built in the footprint of an Elizabethan house and also a Tudor inn called the Cardinal's Hat, dating from around 1570, whose vaulted Tudor cellars survive as the present house's dark and cavernous basement.

No. 49 Bankside, 'The House
by the Thames', which dates
from 1710.

The Cardinal's Hat appears to have started life in the 1570s as a brothel. The house that can now be seen was built in 1710 and its residents included coal and iron merchants, a scrap iron merchant and by 1939 the film director Robert Stevenson (who had a prolific career as a director, making a number of Disney films later in his life). An 'eccentric' civil servant called Sir William Montagu-Pollock was the next person to own the house, followed in turn by the Swedish writer Axel Munthe. In the Second World War the house was lucky to escape serious bomb damage. Today it is a privately owned dwelling, just as it was in 1710. It is not open to the public. The domestic residences of Nos 49–52 Bankside (Grade II listed buildings) are also recognised as remnants of eighteenth-century Bankside.

Further along is the Millennium Bridge designed by Norman Foster and Anthony Caro. The Queen performed the official opening ceremony on 9 May 2000. The bridge was to be opened for public use on 10 June. Hordes of people rushed to cross the bridge anxious to say that they had done so on the first day. The large numbers using the bridge caused it to shake and wobble quite violently. Subsequently the bridge had to be closed to the public. Repairs cost £5 million and the bridge did not reopen until 22 February 2002. Despite the fiasco, the bridge is proving to be immensely popular and has become an accepted and valued part of London's riverscape, connecting St Paul's Cathedral with the impressive Tate Modern building.

An important factor in the regeneration of Bankside was the transformation of Sir Giles Gilbert Scott's Bankside power station into the Tate Modern art gallery. It showed great perception and commitment to convert a disused power station into an attraction that would draw 5 million visitors a year. When the power station closed in 1981 it remained empty for thirteen years until the Tate Modern acquired the site in 1994. In 1995 the leading Swiss architects Herzog & de Meuron were appointed to transform the power station into an art gallery. The final cost was £135 million and on 11 May 2000 Tate Modern opened (with free admission) to the public. The power station had consisted of a substantial central chimney, which stands 99 metres (325 feet) high, and a huge turbine hall, five storeys tall with 3,400 square metres of floorspace that was once home to giant electricity generators. Parallel to the turbine hall was the boiler house, which became the Tate Modern galleries. Further expansion of the building is planned. Tate have embarked on a £215 million development to create a spectacular new building, again designed by Herzog & de Meuron, with the aim of completing it in time for the London Olympics in 2012.

Turn left by Tate Modern and head along Hopton Street, named after Charles Hopton who was born around 1654 and was admitted in his infancy to the freedom of the Fishmongers' Company. On the left hand side at No. 67 is an interesting old house which now looks rather cramped in alongside many of the new developments. This house, with attached railings and old street lamps, was built around 1702.

A few yards further along are the Hopton's Almshouses that were built in 1752 with the assistance of trustees appointed under the will of Charles Hopton. Despite his contribution to the building of the almshouses, he does not seem to have lived in Southwark. He left much of his property to his cousin Thomas Jordan, friends, charities, and the remainder to his sister, Elizabeth. After her death in 1793 the property

Millennium Bridge – the newest bridge to span the Thames connects Tate Modern with St Paul's Cathedral.

Early eighteenth-century house on Hopton Street.

was then left to trustees for the establishment of almshouses in Christ Church. At the first committee meeting held on 10 July 1752, twenty-six 'poor decayed men' of the parish were chosen to occupy the houses. Today the complex includes two garden squares with centre lawns and roses, edged with shrubs. Outside the gates is a drinking fountain and cattle trough. The almshouses were rebuilt and modernised in 1988 and are owned by the Anchor Trust. They are still used for housing and are made available for men and their wives from the Southwark area.

Turn right onto Southwark Street and head towards Blackfriars Bridge. A large Dominican monastery called the Blackfriars, dissolved in the reign of Henry VIII, was formerly sited close to what is now the north-east end of the bridge which takes its name. Almost all physical traces of this monastery have disappeared with the exception of a small section of wall in Ireland Yard, EC4.

The first fixed crossing at Blackfriars was designed by Robert Mylne and opened in 1769. It was the third bridge across the Thames in the then built-up area of London, supplementing the ancient London Bridge. Between 1833 and 1840 extensive repairs were necessary, and a good deal of patching-up was done until at last it was decided to

Hopton's Almshouses, built in 1752 on Hopton Street.

build on the same site a new bridge, which was opened by Queen Victoria in 1869 and still stands today. It is 923 feet long and built to a design by master builder Thomas Cubitt (1788–1855). The bridge was widened between 1907 and 1910 from 21 metres (70 feet) to its present 32 metres (105 feet), making it the widest road bridge in London. Under the arches of the south end of the bridge are a number of mosaics which trace the history of the bridge.

It was under Blackfriars Bridge, early on the morning of 18 June 1982, that the dead body of a man was found hanging from scaffolding. The pockets of his clothes contained bricks and stones – there were even some inside the trousers – and they were clearly intended to weigh him down. There was a large amount of money in his pockets and an expensive watch adorned his left wrist. The deceased was identified as Roberto Calvi, a wealthy and powerful Italian banker with links to the Vatican and to the Mafia. His nickname was 'God's Banker'. His extensive and lucrative operations on behalf of these and other clients had destructively imploded after years during which he had both enriched himself and made huge amounts of money for those who had entrusted their investments to him. He had been convicted of fraud and jailed, but at

Blackfriars Bridge, into which the River Fleet trickles.

the time of his death he was out of prison pending an appeal. The initial conclusion was that he had committed suicide. Later investigations showed that the circumstances of his death rendered suicide impossible. Calvi was in Britain in disguise and with false papers, accompanied by two or three louche characters on whom suspicion immediately fell. Certainly Calvi had reasons to commit suicide. He was disgraced, terrified of the prospect of returning to prison and, perhaps more pertinently, he knew that those whose funds he had badly mismanaged were anxious to meet with him and impress upon him personally their grave displeasure at what, charitably, might be seen as incompetence or, at worst, deliberate deception. The case has never come to any satisfactory conclusion. In 2005 a number of men were tried for Calvi's murder but they were acquitted on the grounds of insufficient evidence.

On the opposite side of the bridge is a magnificently eccentric, wedge-shaped art nouveau pub called The Black Friar. The pub stands very close to where the River Fleet enters the Thames. The Fleet, which was London's second largest river, is now little more than a subterranean storm drain.

10

Marylebone: Oxford Street to Marylebone Road

Marylebone (or St Marylebone), an area once covered by forest and marshland as part of the great forest of Middlesex, evolved from two adjacent manors: the Manor of Lillestone and the Manor of Tyburn. In 1400 the new church was dedicated to St Mary the Virgin (by the bourne) and it was shortly after this that Marylebone replaced the name Tyburn. By the 1720s the growth of Marylebone allowed the *Daily Journal* to comment that people were arriving in London from their country houses in Marylebone. This development in the eighteenth century was associated with certain notable landowners, the Portmans and Portlands, who began to develop fashionable houses and squares to the north of Oxford Street that shaped the identity of Marylebone. Cavendish, Portman, Manchester and Montagu squares are notable examples. The names of various landowners and noble families associated with Marylebone are represented in the streets of the area. Lady Henrietta Cavendish Holles gave her names to Henrietta Street, Cavendish Square and Holles Street; her husband (Edward Harley, 2nd Earl of Oxford) to Harley Street, Oxford Street and Mortimer Street. Landholding tradition in noble families has been maintained in large parts of Marylebone. When the 5th Duke of Portland died in 1879, land passed through the female line to his sister, Lucy Joan Bentinck, widow of the 6th Baron Howard de Walden. The Portland estate then became the Howard de Walden Estate and a great deal of rebuilding took place in the late Victorian and Edwardian period. Today the Howard de Walden Estate owns and leases over 90 acres of real estate in Marylebone, covering an area from Marylebone High Street in the west to Portland Place in the east and from Wigmore Street in the south to Marylebone Road in the north.

Many people will the know the area by some of its well-known landmarks such as Madame Tussauds, Regent's Park, Broadcasting House, the Wallace Collection and, further to the north, London Zoo.

The Walk

This walk is approximately two and a half miles. Opposite Bond Street tube station, across Oxford Street, is Stratford Place. In the thirteenth century a banqueting house was built here for the Lord Mayor and the Corporation of London when they made visits to the conduit which took water from this spot (Tyburn) to the City. The banqueting house was demolished in 1757 and the area was bought by Edward Stratford who built Stratford House at the north end. This is now the Oriental Club, founded in 1824 for gentlemen who had lived or travelled in the east.

Moving east along Oxford Street a few yards from Stratford Place is Marylebone Lane. The meandering course of this road reflects the course of the old River Tyburn. Where the Berkshire Hotel now stands many human remains have been excavated.

Also on Marylebone Lane is Paul Rothe & Son (No. 35) a traditional café-deli dating back to 1900, which sells a wonderful selection of jams and preserves, honey and mustard, English and foreign comestibles.

Continue along Oxford Street and turn left into Vere Street. In July 1810 this was the location of a scandal surrounding the so-called 'Vere Street Coterie', which encapsulated, with a vengeance, the contemporary attitude towards homosexuality. The White Swan, which used to be on Vere Street, was raided by Bow Street police and

The River Tyburn in the mid-eighteenth century.

Paul Rothe & Son's café, established in 1900, on Marylebone Lane.

twenty-three men, described as being of a 'most detestable description', were arrested, including the landlord, James Cooke. The men were found guilty of attempted sodomy and pilloried in the Haymarket. Two other men were executed at Newgate on 7 March 1811. It was estimated that about 40,000 people gathered in the Haymarket – a very violent and unruly crowd who had to come to vent their anger, equipped with various objects to throw. With great vigour they rained down a shower of dead cats, rotten eggs, potatoes and buckets filled with blood, offal and dung, which had been brought by butchers' men from St James's Market. During the next hour of agony, the men walked constantly round the pillory, which was on a fixed axis and swivelled.

Turn right at the end of Vere Street into Henrietta Place and continue past Cavendish Square. First planned in 1717, the building of Cavendish Square was delayed for many years because of the financial crash associated with the collapse of the South Sea Company. Many famous people have lived there, including painter George Romney and Horatio Nelson, while Lord Byron was born at No. 16 Holles Street (now John Lewis) in 1788. In the square is an empty plinth. In 1770 an equestrian statue of Prince William, Duke of Cumberland, 'the butcher of Culloden', was placed there until it was removed in 1868. Only the stone base, complete with its inscription, remains.

Empty plinth in Cavendish Square. It originally held an equestrian statue of Prince William, Duke of Cumberland, 'the butcher of Culloden'.

Continue along Henrietta Place into Margaret Street and then Regent Street. Turn left and walk north. Regent Street eventually merges into Langham Place. All Souls church (consecrated in 1824) stands in the middle of the road. It is unique as the last surviving church built by John Nash. However, the building was not well received in some quarters as a result of its peculiar combination of Gothic spire and classical rotunda. In 1824 in the House of Commons, an MP criticised All Souls as 'this deplorable and horrible object'. More famous is the cartoon which depicts Nash impaled on the spire of All Souls accompanied by a caption which states 'an extinguisher on a flat candlestick'.

To the north east of All Souls is Broadcasting House, headquarters of the BBC, and to the west is the Langham Hotel. The Langham opened in 1865 as the swankiest hotel in London. It has had many famous guests, including Arthur Conan Doyle (1859–1830), Czech composer Antonín Dvořák (1841–1904), Oscar Wilde (1854–1900), actor and playwright Noel Coward (1899–1973), the 1930s Australian cricket team led by Don Bradman (1908–2001) and Mrs Wallis Simpson, who was visited there by the Prince of Wales. In addition, it is reputed to have a number of ghosts, the most famous of which

All Souls church,
Langham Place,
with its once
controversial spire.

seems to reside in room 333. In 1973, BBC announcer James Alexander Gordon was suddenly woken from his sleep by a fluorescent ball floating on the opposite side of the room. As he watched this strange sight, wondering if he was dreaming, the light began to take a human shape. He described the figure as that of an Edwardian gentleman in full evening dress. When Gordon told the story to other staff they confirmed that they had also seen the ghost. In 2003 a female guest left the hotel in something of a premature hurry and without explanation. A few days later the hotel received a letter from her in which she stated that she had been woken in her sleep by inexplicable sounds.

Turn left past the Langham Hotel on to the narrow part of Portland Place and the right into Chandos Street. Located in this street is a fine stuccoed building which houses probably the oldest medical society in the world: the Medical Society of London, which was founded in 1773 by a Quaker physician, Dr John Coakley. The society moved from its home in the City to Chandos Street in 1871.

The Medical Society of London, the oldest medical society in the world, on Chandos Street.

Follow the road into Queen Anne Street. Note the house at No. 2 with the Craigleith stone façade. This is Chandos House, a lesser-known London building. Designed by Robert and James Adams in 1769–1771, Chandos House is one of the finest of the Adams' designs. In 1815 the house was bought by the Austro-Hungarian Embassy, where the first Ambassador, Prince Esterhazy, entertained on such a lavish scale that it eventually led to his ruin. Other titled families took over the lease, including the Countess of Strafford in 1905 and in 1924 the Earl of Shaftesbury, who modernised the property. By 1994 the house was placed on the English Heritage 'Buildings at Risk' Register. The Howard de Walden Estate helped to save the house by buying the lease in 2002 and the Royal Society of Medicine became the owners thereafter. It is now a Grade I listed building and has been restored to its former splendour.

Continue along Queen Anne Street. England's great artist Joseph Mallord William Turner (1775–1851) lived at 23 Queen Anne Street, which is now the site of the Howard de Walden Estate's office. Turner had been a Marylebone resident for forty years at various addresses, including Harley Street, and from 1811 he spent twenty-seven years at Queen Anne Street. Turner built a gallery in this house in 1820 to display many of his masterpieces.

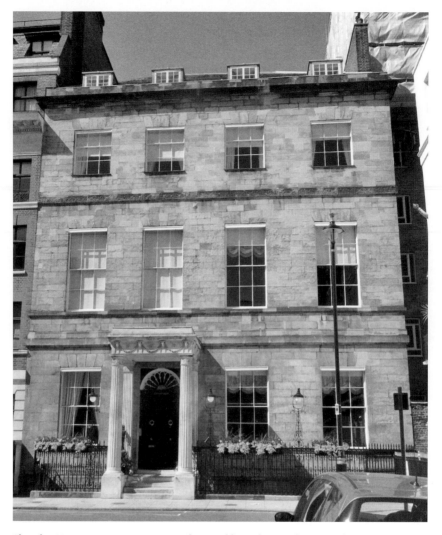

Chandos House, Queen Anne Street, designed by Robert and James Adams.

Queen Anne Street crosses two famous streets: Harley Street and Wimpole Street. Harley Street, named after the landlord Edward Harley, 2nd Earl of Oxford, began its history in 1729, although residents did not arrive until 1752 and it had to wait until after 1770 before development took off more rapidly. It was well placed and fashionable enough to attract wealthy residents. Its association with medical practice in the form of private doctors and consultants would have to wait until the mid-nineteenth century when they started to move into Harley and Wimpole Street. Elizabeth Barrett Browning (1806–1861), the poet, moved with her family to 50 Wimpole Street in 1835.

At the end of Queen Anne Street turn right at Welbeck Street then first left into Bulstrode Street and follow the road to Marylebone High Street and turn right. Marylebone High Street, which was voted best street in London by listeners of

BBC Radio 4, is the focus of the village of Marylebone with its stylish shops, bars and restaurants. The street also follows the course of the River Tyburn, hence its curves.

No. 35 Marylebone High Street is the site of the old Marylebone Gardens, which were opened in 1650 in fields at the back of Marylebone Manor House. No. 35 stands where the entrance to the gardens used to be. The entertainments that took place there included bear-baiting, cock-fighting, bare-knuckle boxing, gambling and bowling. In 1739 Assemble Rooms were added and the gardens became a venue for balls, concerts and fireworks. The gardens were closed in 1778 as a result of the planned residential estates of the Harleys, Portmans and others, and also the mass of complaints from those living in nearby houses about the fire hazard created by plunging fireworks launched during pyrotechnic displays.

Further north is a plaque next to No. 60 Marylebone High Street that marks the site of the Tyburn (later Marylebone) Manor House built around 1250 and rebuilt in 1505. The house was used as a hunting lodge and Queen Elizabeth I stayed there when hunting in Marylebone Park. The Manor House eventually became a school until it was demolished in 1791.

Marylebone High Street joins the very busy Marylebone Road. A few yards along Marylebone Road is an office block (15 Marylebone Road). This is the site of a house where Charles Dickens lived between 1839 and 1851. While here he wrote *The Old Curiosity Shop, Dombey and Son, Martin Chizzlewit, Barnaby Rudge, A Christmas Carol* and *David Copperfield*. Some of the characters from these novels are depicted on a sculptured panel erected in 1960 outside the office block.

On the opposite side of the road is Madame Tussauds and further along is Baker Street Station in which a London Transport memorial records that, 'Beneath this roadway runs the world's first underground passenger railway. It was opened for public traffic by the Metropolitan Railway Company on 10 January 1863.'

Proceed west along Marylebone Road past St Marylebone parish church (where Elizabeth and Robert Browning married in secret in 1846) and turn left into Luxborough Street. Continue as far as Paddington Street and turn right. On both sides of the road (the south side is larger) are Paddington Street Gardens.

In 1730 Edward Harley, the Earl of Oxford, bequeathed land to the south of Paddington Street for use as a burial ground and for the building of almshouses and workhouses. Population increase by the eighteenth century placed greater pressure on the parish churchyard and nearly thirty years later another burial ground was needed. Land was bought from the Portman family on the north side of Paddington Street and the new burial ground was opened in 1772. Among those buried there were many from Marylebone's Huguenot community. This land was known as St Georges Burial Ground and was used from 1731 to 1857 before it was taken over by the municipal authority in 1885 for use as a public garden with Princess Louise officially opening it on 6 July 1886. It was estimated that some 80,000 people were buried in Marylebone burial ground and, while it continues to be a public garden, it is still consecrated ground. There is a statue in the gardens of a 'Street Orderly Boy' (1943), an old name for a street cleaner.

Walk west along Paddington, turn left on to Chiltern Street then left on to Dorset Street and follow the road which then merges into Manchester Street. Cross over Blandford Street (a few yards to the right at 48 Blandford Street is where Michael Faraday, famous for his researches on electricity, was apprenticed to a stationer and bookseller). Cross over George Street.

What was once No. 34 George Street can probably claim to be the site of the first Asian restaurant in London. A coffee house, which offered authentic Asian dishes, was opened here in 1810 by Sake Dean Mahomet to cater for London's many Anglo-Indians. Dean Mahomet, who came from a wealthy family in Bahir, moved to Ireland after a long career in the army and wrote a book in 1794, *The Travels of Dean Mahomet*. He then came to London in 1808 and eventually set up his shop calling it the Hindostanee Coffee House. Despite calling it a coffee house, he did not sell coffee at all. Instead he created a restaurant, but one which provided exotic Indian cuisine. The ambience was reflected in the bamboo-cane sofas and chairs and paintings depicting Indian landscapes. In a separate smoking room, customers could inhale the delights of ornate hookahs (water pipes) containing tobacco blended with Indian herbs. The establishment was advertised in *The Times* as:

HINDOSTANEE COFFEE-HOUSE, No. 34 George-street, Portman square – Mahomed, East-Indian, informs the Nobility and Gentry, he has fitted up the above house, neatly and elegantly, for the entertainment of Indian gentlemen, where they may enjoy the Hoakha, with real Chilm tobacco, and Indian dishes, in the highest perfection, and allowed by the greatest epicures to be unequalled to any curries ever made in England with choice wines, and every accommodation...

Dean Mahomet soon hit financial problems and by 1814 he and his family left for Brighton, where he established himself as a bathhouse keeper and also wrote a book on the art of shampooing. He died in 1851.

Continue along Manchester Street until it merges into Manchester Square. Although a number of famous people have resided in the square – such as Julius Benedict, the German-born composer, who lived at No. 2, and Alfred Lord Milner, the British statesman and colonial administrator, at No. 14 – one of the most eccentric was the religious prophetess Joanna Southcott, who died here in 1814. Her 'revelations' attracted many followers. In 1814, her sixty-fourth year, she learned from her 'Spirit' that she was to have a son, 'by the power of the Most High'. In preparation for her virgin birth and the coming Messiah she had twenty-one doctors to examine her, seventeen of which pronounced her pregnant. The birth, which was to take place in the autumn of 1814, had not happened by November, and Southcott died a month later on 27 December. Her followers remained loyal and explained that the birth was intended as a spiritual rather than a physical event. Southcott left a locked box with instructions that it be opened only in the presence of all bishops at a time of national crisis. In 1928 the box was opened in the presence of a bishop but it revealed nothing of interest. The Southcottian movement still continues in various forms today, including the House of David in America and the Panacea Society of Bedford, England, which owns Southcott's box of sealed writings and also the crib which was made for Joanna's prophesised child, Shiloh.

Manchester Square was built on the Portman estate between 1776 and 1788. The mansion once known as Manchester House and later as Hertford House now dominates the northern side of Manchester Square. It is now the home of the Wallace Collection, a major collection of fine and decorative arts and a magnificent armoury collected in the eighteenth and nineteenth centuries by the first four marquesses of Hertford and Sir Richard Wallace. The 4th Marquess, the greatest of the collectors, spent the last thirty years of his life devoted to collecting works of art such as Rembrandt's *Titus* and Hals's *The Laughing Cavalier,* as well as works by Poussin, Van Dyck, Velázquez, Rubens, Fragonard and many others. He was a reclusive man who had a clear affection for his illegitimate son, Richard Wallace, to whom he bequeathed his collection in 1870 along with over 60,000 acres of property in Ireland. The Seymour family *(marquesses of Hertford)* were outraged and contested the will. It was to no avail and Richard at the age of fifty-two suddenly became a multi-millionaire. But he behaved in a responsible and altruistic way and when he died in July 1890 he left the collection at Hertford House to the nation. In June 1900 the Prince of Wales (the future Edward VII) formally opened the Wallace Collection as a national museum.

11

Bloomsbury

Bloomsbury was developed by the Russell family in the seventeenth and eighteenth centuries into a fashionable residential area. It is notable for its garden squares, literary associations (notably the Bloomsbury Group), and numerous hospitals and academic institutions. Bloomsbury is home to the British Museum, the Royal Academy of Dramatic Art, the British Medical Association, the University of London's Senate House Library and several of its colleges (University College London, Birkbeck, the London School of Hygiene and Tropical Medicine, the School of Pharmacy, the School of Oriental and African Studies and the Royal Veterinary College). Notable hospitals include Great Ormond Street Hospital for children, the National Hospital for Neurology and Neurosurgery, University College Hospital and the Royal London Homoeopathic Hospital.

Bloomsbury can be roughly defined as the square bounded by Gower Street and the lower part of Tottenham Court Road to the west, Euston Road to the north, Gray's Inn Road to the east, and either High Holborn or the thoroughfare formed by New Oxford Street, Bloomsbury Way and Theobalds Road to the south. Bloomsbury merges gradually with Holborn in the south, with St Pancras in the north-east, and Clerkenwell in the south-east. The area's many squares include Russell Square, Queen Square, Bedford Square, Bloomsbury Square, Gordon Square, and Woburn Square. Tavistock Square, home to the British Medical Association, was the site of one of the 7 July 2005 London bombings. The British Museum, which first opened to the public in 1759 in Montagu House, is at the heart of Bloomsbury. At the centre of the museum is the former British Library Reading Room.

The Walk

This walk is almost circular, starting at Tottenham Court Road tube station and finishing at the British Museum. From the station, turn right into Tottenham Court Road then right again at Bayley Street and into Bedford Square.

Bedford Square, built between 1775 and 1780, is the only complete Georgian square left in Bloomsbury. It takes its name from the main title of the Russell family, the dukes of Bedford, who were the main landlords in Bloomsbury. It was in a house near to this square that the Pre-Raphaelite Brotherhood, a group of 'artistic rebels', was founded in 1848. Sir John Everett Millais, along with Holman Hunt and Dante Gabriel Rossetti, formed the Brotherhood in his family home on Gower Street, off Bedford Square.

Bedford College, the first institution to provide female higher education in Britain, was formerly located in (and named after) Bedford Square. It was founded in 1849. In 1900, the college became a constituent school of the University of London and became fully co-educational in the 1960s. In 1985, Bedford College merged with another of the University of London's colleges – Royal Holloway College.

Continue around Bedford Square, stopping at the corner of Gower Street and Montague Place. Gower Street takes its name from Lady Gertrude Leveson-Gower, whose husband was 4th Duke of Bedford. The newly married Charles Darwin (1809–1882) lived for nearly four years (1838–1842) at 12 Upper Gower Street or 'Macaw Cottage'. The house was bombed in 1941 and the site is now part of the Department of Biology, University College London. A modern block called the Darwin Building stands on the exact site of Macaw Cottage.

At 35 Bedford Square lived the surgeon Dr Thomas Wakley (1795–1862), founder of the medical journal *The Lancet* in 1823. Wakley is an interesting character. He became the Radical MP for Finsbury and was in constant trouble with the London teaching hospitals for exposing their nepotistic organisations. He was a coroner who used his position to expose wrongdoing. In 1846 Frederick John White, a soldier, had died from flogging. Wakley's verdict caused a sensation. *The Lancet* provided a means of attacking medical nepotism and malpractice. When he founded the journal he announced, 'A lancet can be an arched window to let in the light or it can be a sharp surgical instrument to cut out the dross and I intend to use it in both senses.'

Continue along Montague Place, turning left at Malet Street. On the right-hand side the large imposing building is the University of London Senate House. At the outbreak of the Second World War, the Senate House became home to the Ministry of Information and the inspiration for the Ministry of Truth in George Orwell's *Nineteen-Eighty-Four* (1949). The building has appeared in a number of films, including the 1995 version of *Richard III, Nineteen Eighty-Four* (1984), *Spy Game* (2001), *Batman Begins* (2005), and *Nanny McPhee and the Big Bang* (2010). For television, the building has featured in *Jeeves and Wooster* (1990–93) and *The Day of the Triffids* (1981).

Continue along Malet Street and turn right at the end (along Byng Place) then stop at the corner of Gordon Square. Writer Virginia Woolf lived at 46 Gordon Square prior to her marriage to Leonard Woolf. Virginia was troubled by recurring mental problems and had to be put under guard several times. She was part of the Bloomsbury Group, or Bloomsbury Set, a group of writers, intellectuals and artists who held informal discussions in Bloomsbury throughout the twentieth century. Among the best known members were Virginia Woolf, John Maynard Keynes, E. M. Forster, and Lytton Strachey. They demonstrated a sexual freedom that was ahead of their time.

Walk along the road and turn left into Tavistock Square. James Burton constructed

Charles Darwin lived in Gower Street from 1838 to 1842.

The imposing University of London Senate House, built between 1932 and 1937.

Plaque near Gordon Square commemorating the Bloomsbury Group.

the buildings on the east side of Tavistock Square, including old Tavistock House (to the rear of the terraced houses). Thomas Cubitt built the northern and southern sides to Tavistock Square, completing them around 1826. The centrepiece of the gardens is a statue of Mahatma Gandhi that was installed in 1968. There is also a memorial to conscientious objectors (unveiled in 1995), busts of Virginia Woolf and Dame Louisa Aldrich-Blake as well as a cherry tree planted in 1967 in memory of the victims of the nuclear bombing of Hiroshima.

Proceed through Tavistock Square, then turn right and continue to Upper Woburn Place. Turn left, cross the road and turn right on Woburn Walk. The Dublin-born poet William Butler Yeats (1865–1939) lived in Woburn Walk between 1895 and 1919. He was a member of the Hermetic Order of the Golden Dawn, a magical order founded in 1888, and based on a heady mixture of Egyptian religion, Judaic mysticism in the form of Kabbalah, and Christian mysticism in the form of Rosicrucianism (a medieval belief system which attempted to provide insight into nature, the physical universe and the spiritual realm).

Proceeding from Upper Woburn Place, turn left and continue along the road back into Tavistock Square and pause outside BMA (British Medical Association) House.

Charles Dickens (1812–1870) moved to London in 1824 and lived in many places around Bloomsbury as well as other parts of London. One of the places in Bloomsbury was part of the old Tavistock House, where he lived between 1851 and 1860. While here he wrote *Bleak House, Little Dorritt, Hard Times, A Tale of Two Cities* and part of *Great Expectations.* BMA House, a stunning Grade II listed building, was originally built in 1911 for the Theosophical Society, an organisation formed in 1875 to advance the spiritual principles of the search for truth known as Theosophy. The society could not afford to complete the house so it was sold to the BMA and opened in 1925.

Continue along Tavistock Square, Woburn Place, to the corner with Russell Square. This square was established in the eighteenth century and named after the surname of the earls and dukes of Bedford. It has links with writers such as T. S. Eliot who worked there when he was an editor at Faber & Faber publishers. There is a blue plaque commemorating him at the north-west corner. Oscar Wilde (1854–1900) spent his last evening in London at 31 Russell Square, before leaving England for good after his release from prison.

Russell Square also has a cabman's shelter, one of the thirteen shelters that still exist. All are now Grade II listed buildings. The Cabmen's Shelter Fund was established in London in 1875 to run shelters for the drivers of hansom cabs and later hackney carriages (taxicabs). A cab driver was not allowed to leave the cab-stand while his cab was parked there. This made it difficult for him to obtain hot meals and could also be unpleasant in bad weather. The Earl of Shaftesbury and other worthies decided to set up a charity to construct and run shelters at major cab-stands. These shelters were small green huts, which were not allowed to be larger than a horse and cart, as they stood on the public highway. Between 1875 and 1914, sixty-one of these buildings were built around London. Most of them were staffed by an attendant who sold food and (non-alcoholic) drink to the cabbies. The attendant was not generally paid, but was expected to make an income from these sales. The shelters were also provided with seats, tables, books and newspapers, most of them donated by publishers or other benefactors. The shelter on the western corner of Russell Square was relocated here from Leicester Square.

Continuing on, pass Guilford Street on the left and Russell Square on the right, until you reach a laneway on the left, called Cosmo Place. Turn into Cosmo Place and proceed through Queen Square to Great Ormond Street.

Great Ormond Street Hospital for Children specialises in the care of children. It was founded in London in 1852, making it the first hospital providing in-patient beds specifically for children. It is known internationally for receiving the rights from J. M. Barrie (1860–1937) to his play *Peter Pan, or the Boy Who Wouldn't Grow Up,* which have provided significant funding for the institution. When the copyright expired at the end of 1987, fifty years after Barrie's death, the UK government granted the hospital a perpetual right to collect royalties on the work (but not creative control). A Peter Pan statue outside the hospital was unveiled on 14 July 2000 by Lord and Lady Callaghan and Tinker Bell was added and unveiled on 29 September 2005 by HRH the Countess of Wessex.

Carry on to the end of Great Ormond Street (the junction with Lamb's Conduit Street.) Turn left and walk to the end of Lamb's Conduit Street. Directly in front, across the road, is Coram's Fields. It is situated on the former site of the Foundling Hospital established by Thomas Coram in 1739 in what was then named Lamb's Conduit Field. It was a place where unwanted children such as street children and orphans could be left. The Foundling Hospital was relocated outside London in the 1920s. However, campaigning and fundraising by local residents, and a donation from the Harmsworth family of newspaper proprietors, led to the creation of the current park which opened in 1936. Coram's Fields is a Grade II listed site.

Go back down Lamb's Conduit Street and note the Lamb public house at No. 94. A beautifully preserved Grade II listed Victorian pub, the Lamb still has the etched glass snob screens in place above the bar. The pub is named after William Lamb, who in 1577 improved upon an existing conduit to bring clean water down from Holborn as an act of charity to benefit the neighbourhood. The Lamb was built around 1729 and still had one of the original wells in the backyard until the early 1900s. It was once the meeting place of the Bloomsbury Group.

Continue to walk along Lamb's Conduit Street. At the junction turn right and go along Theobalds Road, crossing the junction with Southampton Row, at which point the road ahead becomes Bloomsbury Way. Continue along Bloomsbury Way then turn first right into Bloomsbury Square. Bloomsbury Square was one of the earliest London squares, and was developed in the seventeenth century by the 4th Earl of Southampton. It was initially known as Southampton Square. The writer Isaac D'Israeli lived at No. 6

Cabman's shelter in Russell Square.

J. M. Barrie, author of *Peter Pan*, who gifted the play's royalties to Great Ormond Street Hospital.

from 1817 to 1829, and for part of that time his son, the future Prime Minister Benjamin Disraeli, lived with him.

Continue around the square and proceed along Bloomsbury Way to the junction with New Oxford Street, stopping outside St George's church. Nicholas Hawksmoor (1661–1736), a pupil and former assistant of Sir Christopher Wren, designed and built this church between 1716 and 1731. The tower and steeple of St George's is one of Hawkmoor's most inspired dramatic designs. It is based on the Roman author Pliny the Elder's description of the Mausoleum of Halicarnassus (Bodrum, in Turkey). One of the Seven Wonders of the Ancient World, it was famed for its superb sculptures and friezes. St George's, with its pyramidical steeple, is topped by a statue of George I dressed in a Roman toga, which for many years was an object of derision. Like the famed Mausoleum, St George's spire is adorned with sculpture, but major elements of it were removed in a restoration of the 1870s. The lions and unicorns clambering around

Tower of St George's, Bloomsbury, with a lion and unicorn and George I on the steeple.

'Gin Lane' (1751) by William Hogarth. The tower of St George's can be seen in the background.

the base of the steeple are reconstructions, created by the sculptor Tim Crawley and installed on the tower in 2006. The original lions and unicorns were commissioned by Hawksmoor but without the permission of the commissioners, who initially refused to pay for them.

The novelist Anthony Trollope (1815–1882) was baptised at St George's in 1824 and the funeral of Emily Davison – the suffragette who died when she threw herself under the hooves of the King's horse during the 1913 Derby – took place here. St George's tower is depicted in William Hogarth's well-known engraving 'Gin Lane' (1751) in which Hogarth points out the association between excess in artistic style with excess in private manners and morals. Many had been less than flattering about the style of St George's steeple, such as Horace Walpole (1717–1797) who called the building a 'master-stroke of absurdity'. The church was designated a Grade I listed building in 1951.

Walk past the church and turn right along Museum Street. No. 41 Museum Street was the home of Mandrake Press, a small press founded in 1929. In 1930 the company had financial problems and was dissolved. During its short life it published works by the English occultist, ceremonial magician 'The Great Beast' Aleister Crowley (1875–1947). Crowley was responsible for founding the religion of Thelema and was a member of the esoteric Hermetic Order of the Golden Dawn. He gained widespread notoriety during his lifetime and was denounced in the popular press of the day as 'the wickedest man in the world'. At 49 Museum Street is Atlantis Bookshop, one of London's oldest and best esoteric bookshops, which was a popular haunt of Crowley's.

We're now in sight of the British Museum, a good place to finish the walk. Founded in 1753, though the current building dates from the 1820s, it houses the world's largest collection of Egyptian antiquities outside the Egyptian Museum in Cairo. They have formed part of the museum's collection since its foundation. Further antiquities from excavations came to the museum in the late nineteenth century and by 1924 the collection stood at 57,000 objects (that figure has since doubled). Until 1997, when the British Library (previously centred on the Round Reading Room) moved to a new site, the British Museum was unique in that it housed both a national museum of antiquities and a national library in the same building. Famous visitors to the Reading Room have included Lenin and Marx. The Secretum, a name given to Cupboard 55 in the Department of Medieval and Later Antiquities, previously contained the collection of ancient erotica given to the museum by George Witt (1804–1869), physician and collector of phallic antiquities. Inaccessible to the public, it was a repository for exhibits of an erotic nature.

DISCOVER MORE ABOUT
LONDON

ALSO AVAILABLE FROM AMBERLEY PUBLISHING

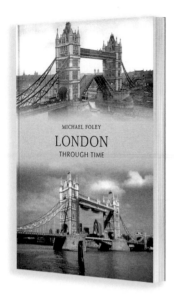

London Through Time
Michael Foley
ISBN 978-1-84868-893-3

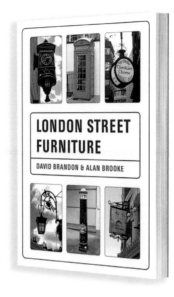

London Street Furniture
David Brandon &
Alan Brooke
ISBN 978-1-84868-294-8

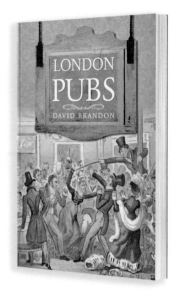

London Pubs
David Brandon
ISBN 978-1-84868-227-6

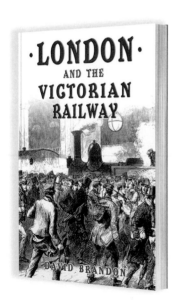

**London and The Victorian
Railway**
David Brandon
ISBN 978-1-84868-228-3

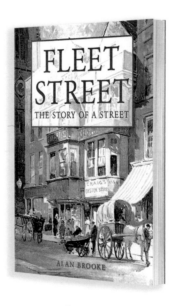

Fleet Street
The Story of a Street
Alan Brooke
ISBN 978-1-84868-229-0

Haunted London
Peter Underwood
ISBN 978-1-84868-262-7

ALSO AVAILABLE FROM AMBERLEY PUBLISHING

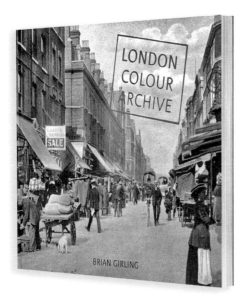

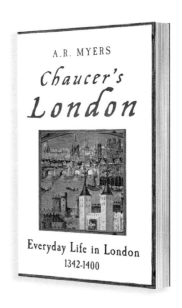

London Colour Archive
Brian Girling
ISBN 978-1-84868-222-1

Chaucer's London
Everyday Life in London 1342-1400
A. R. Myers
ISBN 978-1-84868-338-9

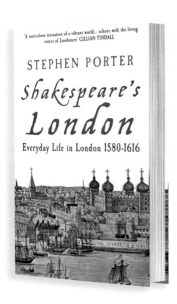

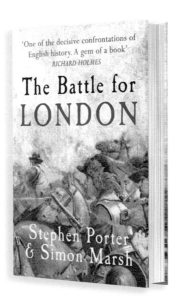

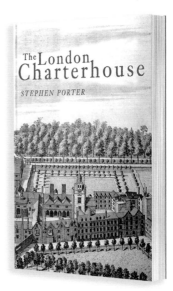

Shakespeare's London
Everyday Life in London 1580-1616
Stephen Porter
ISBN 978-1-84868-333-4

The Battle for London
Stephen Porter & Simon Marsh
ISBN 978-1-8486-8847-6

The London Charterhouse
Stephen Porter
ISBN 978-1-84868-090-6

ENTRY TO THE TRAITORS GATE

www.amberleybooks.com